T0194846

THIS MARKS THE SPOT
WHERE MY PAST RETURNS

JEAN MARKS BAIL

authorHOUSE®

AuthorHouse™
1663 Liberty Drive
Bloomington, IN 47403
www.authorhouse.com
Phone: 1 (800) 839-8640

Published by AuthorHouse 10/21/2019

ISBN: 978-1-7283-3223-9 (sc)
ISBN: 978-1-7283-3224-6 (hc)
ISBN: 978-1-7283-3222-2 (e)

Library of Congress Control Number: 2019916692

Print information available on the last page.

Compiled by Linda Bail Keen

This book is printed on acid-free paper.

September 15, 1926 – June 02, 2019

ABOUT THE AUTHOR

Jean grew up in North Manchester, Indiana during the depression and World War II. She went on to receive an Associate of Arts Degree from Stephens College, Columbia, Missouri, a Business Degree from Indiana University School of Business, and two Master of Education Degrees. She was a member of Tri Kappa Sorority, and St. Luke's United Methodist Church where she attended regularly.

After a career in teaching, Jean volunteered at the Midwest Museum of American Art in Elkhart, Indiana, giving tours to school children and making friends with whom she traveled all over the world.

Her balance, coordination and posture were the result of dance training and enabled her to walk without any assistive devices, ever. Hardships, obstacles and challenges in her life provided the skills and determination to live in and maintain her own home, in Carmel, Indiana where she cared for her precious English Cream retriever, Honey.

CONTENTS

Dedication

With the guidance and the grace of God, your stories are published, Mom. Honey is healthy, happy, and loved. I'm taking good care of her, and she is taking good care of me. Linda

Dorsey P. Bail, Jr., our dad (standing)
Left to Right: Kelsey, Loraine, Linda, Jean Marks Bail

Dorsey P. Bail, Jr. holding Tracey and Jean Marks Bail
Left to Right: Linda, Loraine, Kelsey

Mom's 90th Birthday
Left to Right: Linda, Kelsey, Loraine, Mom, Tracey

Left to Right: Linda, Mom, Loraine, Tracey, Kelsey

DEPRESSION TIMES

"The Great Depression" and I remember when it began. On October 1929 I would have been just three years old. My mother, grandmother and I were sitting at an ice cream table, possibly the one now in my kitchen, at the family drug store.

Our Family Store, North Manchester, Indiana

My father and grandfather walked over. I don't remember what they said but I do remember distinctly my grandmother saying, "We will lose everything."

And my grandfather stated with resignation, "It will be all right. We will get through this."

And they did. My grandfather and father both had great business ability and they worked hard.

At my young age I don't remember a lot during those early years of depression. But I do know that we did not lack basic essentials of living. By sensible spending my family paid off the mortgage on the business and each bought a house. Later my grandfather purchased the store building.

Other people that I knew did not seem to be living any differently than we did and I thought it was normal. Didn't everyone conserve with no waste? Anything broken was patched and repaired instead of replaced. There was actually little variety of items available for purchase. Having something new gave a sense of pride. Most people had a garden to supplement their few grocery purchases. Extra produce helped feed anyone in need.

Family members took care of all other family members. Unemployment was actually not as high as many now believe. Usually someone in the family had a job and sharing was the way to live. Kindness, sharing, and caring were evident everywhere. I don't remember how many times I saw my father hand over a prescription and refuse payment. Doctors and other professionals did likewise. I remember my first grade teacher taking a poorly dressed girl in my class privately into the cloakroom to dress her in clothes she had purchased for her. My girlfriend's mother provided milk for a neighbor child.

People in our small town bragged that no one living there went hungry during the depression times. But everyone worked at any job available even if it was not the desired occupation. There was no unemployment insurance.

Many women sewed their own as well as their children's clothing. Living in a farming area I knew that the feedbags were in prints so that the fabric could be used for clothing or household items. Farm wives would choose the feed to get the desirable pattern.

Carpentry work and shoe repair were important jobs. Many times I walked down Bond Street to the shoe repair shop and waited while my one pair of shoes were resoled or he would replace the worn heels.

Trash collection was unknown. People buried any food not consumed by people or animals. An occasional trip to the dump disposed of all unwanted or unusable items. A trip to the town dump was an exciting adventure with rats scurrying among the debris. Periodically the dump would be burned, usually at night, and the smell was sickening. No thought of pollution.

I now know that depressing conditions were worse in cities than in small towns. Farmers had food but still needed to sell enough to pay taxes, interest on their mortgage, and buy seed and fertilizer. At the time I didn't understand the reasons or politics. But I did hear my father vehemently oppose many of the government solutions to the problems. And I have learned since that he was right on many of them.

There were tramps coming through town on the railroad and this greatly concerned Mother. She said they had a code written under one of the bridges that recorded houses favorable to hospitality. She didn't think we were on the list and was afraid if we were.

But depression days were not all drab and dreary. Saturday nights were social and shopping combined. Farmers came to town and I would know who the farmers were because they always had a white forehead and a sunburned face. They had worn a cap in the fields on the tractor.

Daddy would be working, of course, but Mother would park the car on the street early to get a good spot so she could visit with friends walking by. She would have already done her shopping on a weekday. After the busy Saturday night, Sunday would be church and rest and then another workweek.

Mother (Louise Hoham Marks) and Daddy (Harold Marks)

We had small town street fairs in the summer with the business district crowded with carnival rides, food stands, fortune tellers, and merchants selling merchandise. Sometimes at night, because Daddy worked days, except for Saturdays, we would go to neighboring towns for their fair. The events had been scheduled for various weeks. My parents liked the taffy which came in a variety of colors and flavors. It was still being sold at the State Fair last year.

Movie theaters were important. We had two theaters in town -- the Ritz and the Marshall, named after Vice-President Marshall who was born in a house at that location. The Ritz specialized in cowboy movies and B rated presentations. The classier films were shown at the Marshall—"Gone With the Wind", "Wizard of Oz."

I remember as an infant, sitting on my father's lap watching Al Jolson sing in the first sound movie. Daddy said, "This is historic!" How far we have come!

Movie theaters always had a sign in front each summer that said, "Cool Inside!" It was the only place anywhere with air conditioning and they kept it freezing cold to prove it.

Wednesday night was "Bank Night." One needed a ticket to claim the prize and someone might proudly win as much as $50 which was a lot in those days. The theater manager would draw the winning ticket at the end of the movie. If no one produced the ticket, the amount would be raised for the next Wednesday. There were some who would buy a ticket but only appear for the drawing and not attend the show. This always seemed stupid to me.

Saturday afternoon movies were good baby sitters. For 15 or 25 cents children could attend and this included a snack. I don't remember having anything to drink -- just popcorn or candy.

In my junior high years we had a skating rink which was wonderful in cold weather. We all learned to do all kinds of fancy tricks and dances to the music. I always had to wear the rental skates even though most of my friends had their own pair. Some music still reminds me of the happy hours at the skating rink.

The depression had a lasting effect on my life. It wasn't that my family suffered from hunger or cold or deprivation of any kind. But it was in the way everyone lived. There was no waste.

"If you aren't going to be in the room, you do not leave the light on! Go back and turn it off!" How many times did I hear that!

"Close the door! You're not living in a barn!"

"Close the door! We can't heat the outside!"

"The refrigerator door can only be opened for a very short time."

"Don't throw that away. You may need it later."

So how did we pack rats get to be that way? We lived during the depression when things were not affordable and during WWII when they were not available.

HABLA ENGLISH ANYBODY? --- PLEASE!

"I'm sure this is the bus the concierge at the hotel told me to use. But it doesn't look like a tourist area."

I staggered out of my seat to approach the bus driver for assurance. I asked and he nodded and smiled. "No English."

Struggling back to my seat as the bus moved I asked those around me. "No English." I wisely had not depended on my year of college Spanish and searched for the tourist Spanish handbook in my bag. I had purchased this item for the trip. Since I wasn't ordering food or asking for the restroom it was of little help. Obviously, the writer had never been on a city bus in Acapulco, Mexico wondering if she would ever see home in the USA.

The bus moved on up a winding mountain road. Small houses disappeared and we were in the midst of shacks with clotheslines in the yards filled with laundry.

I thought, "Well, it will turn around and go back and I'll see the hotel." Even in the summer heat, I remember thinking how clean and pleasant the passengers were. When I asked if anyone spoke English they would just smile and shake their heads. I was too complacent.

The worst was yet to come!!

The rickety bus reached the top of the shabby residential area. And its motor went completely dead!!

We passengers didn't need a common language to feel and look the distress. I thought, "There is absolutely no way out of here." This was before cell phones and these people weren't likely to have telephones in these shacks. I couldn't even see an electric wire. So we all sat there and sat there for what seemed an eternity!

The bus driver appeared not disturbed. He got out of the bus, looked around until he saw a couple teenagers, and motioned to them. They got behind the bus, and started pushing it along, and then the motor loudly clicked in! The boys hopped on for probably a free ride.

I didn't know where I was, but we did start to ride though a more prosperous area and what looked like a school. I started asking those who boarded the bus if they spoke English. One well dressed gentleman told me in very broken English to get off, cross the street, and take the next bus from there, and I would reach my hotel, and I did.

Many times I have been lost in the United States and in foreign countries as well. But just once on the top of a mountain in a poor section of Acapulco, Mexico.

A STRANGE ENCOUNTER

"Mother, I don't think we should do this."

"Don't worry. It will be fun. I've been on many city buses. We take just one bus to the park and then I'll call a taxi for the return trip so we can be on the next train."

My older son, Kelsey, may have had a premonition of problems to come.

We stood outside the famous St. Louis Union Train Station where I had been many times as a college student in Missouri. I had already checked our four small suitcases, one for each of the three older children and another for the youngest child and myself. We were on a summer vacation visit with their father's parents.

left to right – Loraine, Jean, Tracey, Kelsey, Linda

Five hours in a train station with four children aged four to ten, I knew, would be miserable. They had already tired of the games and puzzles from our first train trip from northern Indiana.

St. Louis Zoo in Forest Park, then, as now, has a well deserved reputation as one of the best in the country. We had a lovely afternoon in beautiful summer weather. Because it was before cell phones, I asked for pay phone locations. This was pointed out to me and we walked wearily in that direction. The sign on the phone read: "Out of Order." We walked on to the next phone. Same sign. By this time I was carrying, Tracey, the four year old, and the other three seemed ready to drop.

I looked around the beautifully landscaped lawns of the park and saw no one to ask for help. I wondered how we could possibly be on time to board our next train to the other side of Missouri where the grandparents would be expectantly awaiting the arrival of their only grandchildren.

Then an old car approached, occupied by two young black fellows. They stopped.

This was in the sixties and I had been watching the race riots in cities across the country on our old black and white TV. Young guys like these were carrying signs, setting fires, and doing all kinds of damage. I felt as though I had been hit by a stun gun.

Both got out of the old sedan. One black youth leaned on the hood and the other asked about my problem.

I told him and just stood there frozen.

"I know what you're thinking, but it's all right. We'll help you."

What to do. No real choice. I said, "All right."

The five of us crowded into the back seat of the vehicle and he asked which door at the train station. I told him the main one and offered to pay him the taxi fare.

They helped us all out of the back seat and he said, "I don't want paid. I'm just glad I could help you."

Angels of all kinds can appear anywhere and don't wear wings.

USE IT UP -- WEAR IT OUT

"Grandma, they're ringing the bell. I think somebody wants to buy strawberries." I jumped from the rope swing in the yard as Grandma hurried out of the house drying her hands on her apron as she walked toward the front yard.

"Lawsy me. I thought I would have these strawberries stemmed for jam before I had to stop."

I would stand at the edge of the homemade roadside produce stand with the bell on one end as Grandma weighed up the food items on a hanging scale at the other end. She would add up the sale on scrap paper and accept the payment into her apron pocket. Purchases were wrapped in newspaper or placed carefully in precious paper sacks. Regular customers brought their containers.

Then we would return to the kitchen, my favorite room in the old farm house. Jars lined the table with paraffin ready to melt for sealing the jars of strawberry jam.

The kitchen had a dish cupboard in one corner with the table in front, a baking cupboard in another corner, a sink with running water and a pump in one corner, and a stove which was coal fired in the winter, so the kitchen was always warm then. They changed to a summer stove in the spring.

My grandparents were what they called city farmers because their house with acreage was located at the edge of town.

When my mother and her two sisters were growing up there, their land would produce almost all of their food. And it still did. In addition to the produce and chickens that I knew, in those days they had a cow in the barn and pigs in the pig sty.

Now the chicken coop was the active establishment and the garden was almost a fourth of the property. Beyond the fruit orchard and a field they leased to a farmer for corn, were the Pennsylvania Railroad tracks which were very busy in those days.

I would go to sleep in the big feather bed in the upstairs west room. I was told to listen for train whistles. Grandma would walk me up to see the trains the next day, but I wasn't allowed to do that on my own.

We would walk down the sidewalk, which at one time led to the now extinct outhouse, past the barn which once housed a cow in addition to Grandpa's old box style Chevy.

The chicken house was on the left filled with chickens, then the empty pig sty on the right. We would walk through the orchard which sometimes had apples on the trees. Train after train would pass by. We would stop at the large garden on the way back to the house to pick or pull some items to carry to the kitchen. The garden was huge and fenced in with an entrance gate near the house yard. Lilacs sent a pleasant aroma in the spring. And in the summer we could pause at Grandma's morning glory house. Grandpa had made a metal frame behind the woodshed and she had laced strings so that the flowers made a bower of blue blooms to admire from the outside and to enjoy inside.

I never remember seeing a grocery store can of anything. Fruits and vegetables were canned as they ripened. Later they rented a "locker" in town so that some of the food could be frozen. I still remember the windmill and wood shed behind the house, but they slowly disappeared.

My grandparents could have posed for American Gothic paintings.

Mother's Parents

Grandma always wore long sleeved house dresses, heavy cotton stockings, and sensible shoes. She wore a sunbonnet outdoors. She had never in her life

11

had her hair cut and she wore it in a twisted bun on the back of her head and washed it in rain water. She most often wore an apron.

Grandpa wore cotton shirts and cotton pants with suspenders. The pants always looked big as though they really needed to be held up. Sometimes there were patches on his clothing. I think that when he had worked in his younger years it was as a salesman.

In fact, my grandparents had met when my grandmother worked as a bookkeeper in her father's hardware store and the new young salesman, my grandfather, started working there, too.

Their oldest daughter was married and lived with her family on a farm in the area. My mother left home for nurse's training in Indianapolis, married my father, a pharmacy student, and moved to a town 50 miles away.

Their youngest daughter still lived at home and worked in an office in town. It was close enough to home that she could walk to work. But I remember her helping at home, too. I helped her pick strawberries and when I only wanted to pick the big ones I was instructed, "Pick clean so the plants will produce longer." A rule: her room upstairs was off limits to children.

Throughout elementary school I would always stay with my grandparents for a week or more after school was out for summer vacation. And it was always strawberry time.

Mornings I would hurriedly dress and use the bathroom upstairs, the only one in the house, and then sit at the kitchen table for breakfast. It was always the same. Grandma soaked wheat grains. Grandpa and I would each eat a bowl of that with milk and sugar. Then I would follow him to the garden. He successfully grew all vegetables and plowed with an old hand plow which he pushed down the rows. And I followed behind. I remember his irritation if insects invaded his territory. He would squeeze bugs between his fingers while I squirmed with distaste. The next day I would see a white or yellow powder covering the foliage.

Grandpa's skills were in many areas. He could build a box kite from scratch with scrap materials and it would fly. He would always throw the long rope over a limb in the walnut tree in the back yard and install the wooden seat that he had made. How many happy hours I spent in that swing. When I was younger he had pulled me around the yard in the little Studebaker wagon with the seat on top.

In summer Grandma did the laundry outside on the sidewalk beside the back porch. I liked to grind the wringer handle but I was careful not to get my fingers near the rollers as instructed. Then we would hang clothes on the clothes line.

I helped and learned other homemaking skills. Shelling peas was a long tedious job but the fresh peas were worth the effort. Preparing green beans was another activity.

Grandma's fun time was doing needlework and I worked hard learning embroidery. I embroidered quilt squares that my grandmother made into a doll quilt, still one of my cherished possessions.

Sometimes I would sit in the parlor by the old upright piano with the blue and white vases on top that I loved and listen to the thick scratchy records on the old wind up Victoria.

Grandpa enjoyed listening to Chicago ball games on the radio. I never remember either grandparent reading for recreation.

Our meals often included chicken and fresh eggs which also were produced on the farm. The chickens had a house covering a third of the coop. All garbage was thrown into the chicken yard which was supplemented by regular chicken feed. Grandpa would clip a section of wing off any chicken that might "fly the coop." And Grandpa would chop the heads off as many as were needed for meals. The body would flop around. I cringed in sympathy for the poor chicken. Then Grandma would do her routine of cleaning the chicken. I absolutely and completely avoided this procedure. Grandma also gathered eggs every morning. The chickens nested on shelves in their house. Chickens had been purchased as tiny chicks and were kept peeping in the boxes by the kitchen wood stove while they were young.

I had many cringing moments. Both of my grandparents wore "false teeth" as most people of their generation did. Grandma would remove hers at the kitchen sink, rinse them under the faucet and then replace them in her mouth. I would stand by and watch this procedure with wonder and distaste.

I always visited at circus time in the summer and it was a special time. I would look out the upstairs east window in the evening at an empty field. The circus train would magically appear in the night on the Pennsylvania Railroad track siding and looking out that same window in the morning there would be a huge circus tent, animals, and many busy people.

Grandma insisted on breakfast before she would take me through the garden to the fence that separated the properties. The circus people were all busy at work as were the elephants. Town boys carried buckets of water with a ticket to the circus as their pay.

In the afternoon we watched the circus parade and the next afternoon we could go to the circus itself. One year we sold candy bars at the produce stand.

I would go to sleep with the circus sounds of the evening performances which were considered too late for children. They drowned out the train sounds.

Then the circus would magically pack up and leave just as mysteriously as it had appeared.

In recent years I have realized what miserable lives the circus people and animals suffered. But in those childhood years it was magic and I was fortunate to have been so close to it.

Grandma seldom left the house and it took a long time for her to get ready for a downtown trip when my mother would visit and take her.

When they went to the World's Fair in Chicago with us, Grandma carried a shopping bag with her home away from home including medications and toilet paper. I remember them sitting along the walkway a lot, completely out of their element. But Grandma had been to the 1893 Chicago World's Fair in her youth.

Family get-togethers were a frequent occasion, particularly on holidays. The meal was always chicken, of course, with various vegetables. The adults ate in the dining room with the children in the kitchen noisily picking at each other. After the food had been passed around the dining room table for adults, someone would bring to the kitchen whatever was left for the children. I loved the strawberry shortcake with real whipped cream.

Sometimes the adults would play card games on the dining room table after the women did all the clean up, visiting with each other as they worked. There were children activities also. A girl who was a couple of years younger than me lived next door and was a frequent playmate. All of the children in the neighborhood, residents and other visiting relatives, happily played hide and seek, sometimes in the dark, while adults sat on the front porch visiting. There were many hiding places, particularly good at night. We also caught "lightning bugs" to put in jars and then left the lids off so they could escape after we had fallen exhausted in bed.

One bug I could not endure was a mosquito. They particularly liked my fair skin and would swarm around me. I was always covered with bites, sometimes swollen ones. I don't remember ever having medication for the itching even though Grandma had her secret homemade salve which eased many ailments.

Not long ago I drove down Pennsylvania Avenue. The farm acreage is now a housing development. The tree that held the swing is gone. The barn is gone. The house has been remodeled and changed. But the happy childhood memories are a gift that is immeasurable.

CAR TALK

"And the speed limit was 35 miles per hour."

"You mean in town."

"I mean everywhere. After all, these were war years and everyone willingly, if not happily, complied to war regulations."

"But the cars in those days probably didn't go any faster anyway."

"Oh, yes, they did. Before the war there were fewer cars, narrow two lane highways, and poor safety features of any kind. Seat belts were unknown. Cars had running board ledges on the sides and boys would stand on them for a ride. Train crossings were a particular hazard because the trains ran frequently and speeding in front of them was often fatal."

My older son, Kelsey, and I were discussing cars "in the old days" before his occupation was eventually in the car business.

During the entire war we drove the same 1941 Buick sedan. Everyone drove the same old car for the duration. New cars were not available. Car parts and new tires were not available. Gas was rationed. We had a B card because of my dad's business but most people had an A card. Gas mileage on cars was not good.

We were able to take our alternate Sunday visit to Plymouth to visit my mother's family but at 35 mph the 50 mile trip seemed unending. We occasionally made the 35 mile shopping trip to Fort Wayne. Merchandise in the stores was skimpy. I was able to receive my three pairs of shoes per year (these were rationed). I was always assigned the sensible leather oxfords with soles that could be replaced. Later I could have leather loafers or saddle shoes but they had to have repairable soles. Since we walked everywhere in town, good shoes were a necessity.

Daddy loved cars. Before the war he traded cars almost every year. He had one of the first car radios, an exciting innovation. I remember listening to "The Shadow" and other mysteries on our way home from Plymouth on Sunday evenings.

We heard about the bombing of Pearl Harbor on the car radio on our way home from Chicago on Sunday, December 7, 1941. The next day we heard on the home radio the president talk about "the day that would live on in infamy." And it has.

Daddy always took excellent care of his cars. They had to be clean inside and out. We ate or drank absolutely nothing in the car. I remember sneaking a small candy bar one time undiscovered. The worst hunger time was on our way to Plymouth for the Sunday dinner. Daddy always kept the store open on Sunday morning until noon "in case someone needed medicine." So our dinner at the grandparents' house would be at 1:30 or 2:00. I remember feeling physically ill waiting so long for food.

My parents bragged about the good condition of their cars for trade in. They said that there were people waiting to buy their second hand car while they drove a new one.

Buying gas was easy. The driver simply drove into the filling station and rolled down the driver's window unless it was summer and the window would already be down because there was no air conditioning. Then a fellow from the station would appear and ask how much. He would put the gasoline in the tank and check the oil and wipe the windshield clean for no extra charge. Gas was about 12 or 15 cents a gallon. The attendant would also check the tires and provide free maps if requested.

Cars lacked many features we take for granted such as automatic transmission. All drivers used the clutch and gear shift. And there were no turn signals. To turn left the driver needed to crank down the window and point their left arm left. To turn right that same arm pointed up and to the right. With no seat belts, small children might stand up riding in the back seat supporting themselves on the back of the front seat which, of course, had no head rest.

Those fortunate enough to have a garage operated the side opened door by hand. And a gravel grease pit would be located under the car so that drippings would not damage the floor.

We went many places in those old cars before the war changed everyone's lives. Long trips were not as successful for my parents as shorter ones. I vaguely remember a quick vacation trip around Lake Michigan and another to the Smokey Mountains in Tennessee.

But we went to Chicago on many occasions. My father's uncle and aunt lived in a small modest rental on Clark Street. The area is now new and high rent. We stayed with them on trips to the Chicago World's Fair in 1933 and 1934.

We went to area trade shows for the business -- Chicago, Fort Wayne.

I really liked the one at the Spink-Wawasee Hotel in Syracuse, Indiana. The shows would always have snacks, toys, and treats. The view of the lake from the hotel was gorgeous. Of course, I always had to be dressed up in hat, gloves, purse, and fancy dress for the occasion. I guess we were supposed to look successful.

But Indianapolis was a more frequent destination. Mother had graduated from nurses' training at the Methodist Hospital there and Daddy from Pharmacy School, later affiliated with Butler University. When Mother graduated, she was a head nurse in the emergency room. Race car drivers were brought to that emergency room in an ancient truck ambulance after their frequent accidents on the old Indy 500 track and Mother made friends with many of them. So, after my parents moved away, in addition to visiting school friends in Indianapolis, they would yearly return for the Memorial Day race. I remember coming with them on occasions, either to the race or the trials and sitting on the old wooden bleachers. We cheered when the speeds reached 112 mph. Safety features were meager and accidents with injuries and even deaths were expected.

Daddy would park in a garage in downtown Indianapolis and we would take a bus to the track. Someone in the track parking lot might damage his car in some way and he took no chances.

Mother packed box lunches for each of us and we had a cold bottle of Coca Cola to drink. I always slept all the way home and then staggered in to bed after begging to sleep in the car all night.

The 1946 race was particularly memorable. We were returning from Columbia, Missouri where I had been in school and went to the race on the way home. The track had been closed during the war and then resold to the Hulman family of Terra Haute, Indiana. This was exciting because it was the first race after the war.

Our seats were directly behind the pits and we could almost help the mechanics because we were so close. Spectators are not allowed to even be near that area today. Mother had always maintained that speed in the pit stop often made a difference in the outcome of the race.

Then, Gasoline Alley was wooden sheds, no fear of terrorism, no restrictions on what you carried to the track. But one BIG difference! People dressed as though they were going some place special. They had been through a depression and a world war and they didn't want to look sloppy or poor.

Before the war people dressed up to go places as well. I wore a hat and gloves at a young age. There was pride in looking your best no matter what your circumstances. Then during the war, clothing was difficult to purchase. We had one small department store in town and they would buy the same style in various sizes. Women seeing friends in the same dress was a common occurrence and they would just laugh about it. There was little to laugh about in those years.

I find myself rebelling about some of those early times. My car is for transportation. My dogs ride in the back seat. I use the cup holder and occasionally eat food in the car if I so desire. And, before a late lunch, I eat a snack even if it might "spoil my lunch."

I dress casually for many occasions without a hat and gloves. I seldom see someone in the same dress. But when I did once a few years ago, we laughed about it just as my mother and her friends had done.

TRAGEDIES OF THE TIMES

"It's very bad news." My mother hung up the receiver on the wall telephone with a sad face and tears in her eyes. I lay down the spoon in my bowl of corn flakes.

"Your friend Betty Jean died early this morning."

"What do you mean?"

"She has gone to heaven to live with the angels and you won't see her on earth again."

"But I was just playing with her yesterday. We played tag in her front yard."

The seven and eight year old girls, her classmates, were all flower girls at her funeral wearing their best Sunday dresses. I remember each of us carrying flowers to place on her casket. But I remember most hearing her mother crying and calling out repeatedly, "My baby, my baby."

Betty Jean had died needlessly of appendicitis.

We faced other childhood deaths. Bill Reed died of polio in the big epidemic. All young people had been quarantined in their homes that late summer and the start of school had been postponed.

Polio season in the fall was always a scary time. Mother kept us away from crowds and we never went to the State Fair which sounded like fun.

We collected dimes in little March of Dimes cans. The crusade was successful but not soon enough to save poor Bill.

Jack Grossnickle was another lost child who could have been saved by our current surgery. He had a heart condition and for awhile attended school part time. But then he was resigned to only watching us out of his house window as we ran and jumped and played on our way to school. He must have sadly known that his life span was to be short.

Ann Stauffer lived only four short years. She was a beautiful little girl but had a bluish cast to her skin from a heart defect. She, too, might have lived longer with our current heart surgery.

The death that affected me the most was my grandfather's death when I was twelve. He had a heart attack and I would sit on his bed and talk. Bed rest was the supposed cure in those days. I don't know whether he also was prescribed medicine of any kind. But I do know that he and my grandmother did not change their high fat, sugar, starch diet. He had a second heart attack and was gone.

These people all died untimely deaths. If medical research had progressed faster it could have made a difference.

WOMEN OF INFLUENCE

"This is where you need to go to college." Mrs. Oppenheim laid a packet of brochures on the soda fountain counter. "Our Barbara went there." I continued preparing the ice cream sundaes for her and her husband as I had many times. They lived in a large house at the edge of the business district and would walk the short distance for dessert in the evenings.

I gave a casual glance at the papers. "I'm going to talk to your parents about this," she continued.

Mr. Oppenheim had been talking to my father and they were laughing at something that had happened in town. Not really a lot to laugh about in those war times. He and his father operated the only small department store in town.

After they left I looked at the brochures. Columbia, Missouri? Where was that? I had always been a good student and rather assumed I would attend the small local college with some of my high school classmates. Then, of course, I would still be dipping ice cream as I had been doing most of my life.

Was it possible that I would be traveling cross country on a train in a sleeper car in war time to a college I had never seen? But I did!

Valerie Oppenheim did persuade my parents to send me to Stephen's College and it made a huge difference in my life.

Stephens College, Columbia, Missouri

Irene Stauffer was another local lady who helped me grow up. She suggested a summer camp in northern Michigan and I went for two complete summers in junior high years. I learned more there than the swimming, canoeing, sailing, hiking. I learned crafts and proper table manners while eating a variety of foods I had never before even seen.

Elta Fultz lived across the street from us and I spent a lot of time in her home. Her husband was a car salesman and they had no children. I picked hollyhocks in their yard and climbed their two cherry trees in season. And I could eat as many as I wanted. She would suggest, "Pick some to take home for your mother to bake in pies." But Mother didn't bake pies so I didn't do that.

Mildred Schmedel was my neighbor and friend. I know she helped me get into Tri Kappa sorority before I went away to college. In that way I was introduced to many of the ladies in town I had barely known. It helped me in later years when I moved to other Indiana locations.

My girl friend's mother, Lucille Urschel, had tremendous influence on my life. I spent unending hours in their home. She would call my mother any time she felt my needs were not being met in any way. And I went with them to basketball games many times.

My parents were not interested in any sports except auto racing. Mother always said she was not allowed to go to basketball games because, "Papa said they didn't wear enough clothes." And Daddy had been involved in music activities. He played cornet in the Peru High School band.

These five small town women were instrumental in helping me grow up. Their husbands were in a variety of occupations -- newspaper editor, factory owner, banker, store owner, car salesman. I know I never thanked them in person. But I have never forgotten them.

A MESSAGE OF LOVE

"I don't know how I can do this."

"But, Mother, you have to. You know you have always wanted the best for Mitzi. And this just has to be."

The veterinarian directed us to the examining room and an assistant wheeled my darling red golden retriever in on a surgical cart. I hugged her and cried my heart out into her furry neck. She was heavily medicated but managed to weakly lift her tail once. My daughter, Linda, also tearfully stroked her face.

"You need to leave now. We'll take care of her." The doctor's wife, also a veterinarian, directed us out the back door.

We got in my daughter's car. "You know, I have much to be thankful for. We had ten good years together. She wasn't sick long, at least to my knowledge, and I didn't get up in the morning and find her dead." In fact, I had been in contact with the doctor for a few days and had been following the treatment prescribed until she got worse and needed to make the trip to the office.

I cried and cried and cried. My daughter said she cried more over Mitzi than some of our relatives and it wasn't even her dog.

We put away her bed and toys but that didn't help to ease the pain of losing Mitzi. Everything reminded me of her. I remembered how I had carried her home from the house next door where her mother and sister still live. I took the tiny little thing with me everywhere I could. She picked out her toys at the supermarket hidden in my jacket.

My dog didn't sleep in her especially chosen crate for long because she liked my bed better. But when I later bought a new mattress for myself and a little bed for her next to mine she was compliant.

The little dog had full run of the house at an early age and she was a mischievous puppy. She liked dish towels, socks and shoes. She once destroyed my favorite watch. Later, full grown, she would tease by running around the house with those items but didn't damage them.

Mitzi, early on, claimed the back seat of my car and, as a puppy, rode on the ledge looking out the back window. She rode in the back seat of three vehicles in her lifetime and adjusted to each. In fact, when I moved and only had a small spot for her, she adjusted without complaint. When I would park and walk her to a grassy spot she had no trouble doing what she was there for. And if I would leave her in the car just long enough to use a rest room or pick up coffee, she would sit in the driver's seat, ready to drive. And if I had a bagel with the coffee, she expected a bite and was successful.

Mitzi liked to eat her meals when I ate mine and would remind me if I didn't fill her dish. In fact, she could make sounds that sounded like words and I actually understood what she was saying.

Mitzi

My dog was friendly to all, particularly to those who called her "pretty girl" and she was just that with her beautiful copper red coat. But she had many fears -- balloons, flags, vacuum cleaner, loud noises, and workmen carrying a ladder or tool box. She would greet them cheerfully until she saw their equipment.

Her favorite activity was walking and we walked many places together. She always stopped at crossings to look for traffic and would patiently wait if I needed to tie my shoe string. We walked the neighborhoods and in numerous parks. We walked the Indianapolis Circle at Christmas time and enjoyed the holiday lights.

But she loved walking the Monon Trail the best and walked with her head up as though it was her own special place. No other dog or person could change her concentration. We walked the trail to the Carmel Farmer's Market a number of times and she glowed in the adoration of people there. She loved wearing a bandana around her neck and didn't like having it removed even to change to a clean new one.

Mitzi had many experiences in her life time. She sat under my folding chair between my legs at the Blueberry Festival parade in Plymouth because she didn't like the sound of the bands. She sat with me for two hours at the License Bureau and enjoyed having the other waiters pet her. She walked the Elkhart Dog Walk two times and won door prizes the first year. She stayed with me when I would house sit for my cousin in Plymouth. She went with me to my girl friend's home in Ohio. She checked out the dance studio in Mishawaka. She visited a nursing home in Elkhart on different occasions. She ran twice in the Westfield run with Linda and knew when the gun sounded that it was time to run and win so she would urge Linda uphill. And they did win once and she wore the medal around her neck for a photo.

Linda/Mitzi

She sat in the Westfield school cafeteria, ordinarily off limits for dogs. She enjoyed sleeping in the guest room at Linda's and in tormenting the cats. At my other daughter's home, she loved to run at the farm teasing the horses as they watched her in fascination. She went with me to a church retreat and we walked the lakeside and woods and shared the small cabin room overnight.

My dog knew that when I packed a certain bag that we were going somewhere overnight and she would sit by it ready to get in the car. But she did need to be boarded many times when I couldn't take her and the attendants acknowledged how good she was and what a joy to have her with them.

One late afternoon, a few days after I had lost Mitzi, I answered the phone. "I'm your neighbor down the street and I have some flowers for you that were mistakenly delivered to me by the florist."

"Tell me where you live and I'll walk down and get them."

"I'm just leaving the house. I do know where you live and I'll bring them by."

I walked out to the sidewalk in front of my house and, holding back tears, was telling friends walking by that I had had to give up Mitzi. They walked on and a lady drove up in a little red car. She parked and walked over to me and handed me a florist wrapped vase with sun flowers and an envelope.

"This is probably from my children," I explained. "They feel badly that I have had to lose my dog."

She stepped back, stared at me, and held up her hands, palms facing toward me. "Your dog is still with you. I see her love encircling you." She stepped back slightly.

"Are you, are you psychic?"

"This love is so strong. It can't be missed. She wants me to tell you that she is fine and doesn't want you to be so sad and to cry all the time. And she'll help you get another dog."

I stood in the yard, clutching the vase, motionless, silent, and unbelieving.

"I need to go. I'm late for an appointment," the lady explained and got in her car and drove away.

I walked into my house in a daze. But a strange thing happened. I felt a weight lifted of my shoulders. I had loved my darling Mitzi so much. And I know she felt the same.

I really believe that she did send me a message in this strange way. This was no coincident. The flowers were from the veterinary office and they also made a donation for animal research at Purdue University in her name. They apologized for the flowers being delivered to the wrong place. And they had not ordered the vase which was the color of Mitzi's fur.

A few months later the phone rang. "Mother, I came home from work a different way, Linda told me, and there was a sign in front of a lane in this nice area. It said, 'Golden Retriever Puppies' with a phone number. I called and checked it out with a friend of mine. You go by tomorrow and pick out a puppy. They are darling and your children are buying you one."

"I thought I would wait longer before getting another dog. I had this surgery on my foot. I want to take another trip. No dog can replace Mitzi"

No excuse was successful and when I saw the sweet little things the next day my resistance disappeared. Then I couldn't decide which of the two smallest, precious, white female puppies to take home. So, now I have two.

Flora and Lilly

One is a reincarnation of Mitzi with her same personality and her twin sister is the mischievous playmate that Mitzi didn't have. They have both filled a special place in my heart. But my darling Mitzi will never be forgotten.

ALL IN THE NEIGHBORHOOD

The thirties, depression time, hard times, but it was a different world in small town Indiana. Everybody knew everybody and took an interest in everybody's welfare. Many of us children lived happy carefree lives. Doors weren't always locked and grownups looked out for all the children.

We moved in to the small new house on Third Street in 1930 when I was four and I sadly sold it fifty six-years later.

In those early years the neighborhood was a child's paradise. The sidewalks were new and smooth for roller skating. Our driveway had a concrete hill to the street crossing the sidewalk which made a running start for skating down the sidewalk. Daddy would adjust my skates each spring so the clamps would fit over my shoes and I wore a skate key on a lanyard around my neck so that I could loosen and tighten the skates on my leather soled shoes. We would roller skate to school in pleasant weather and line our skates up in the hall. No thought of theft and to my knowledge it never happened.

We played hop scotch on that same smooth sidewalk.

In early spring we would also fly kites on the lot next to the house. I had a regular short wooden stake to figure eight the line and with unending string the kite would become just a little dot in the distant sky. Of course then it would take a long time to wind the kite back in -- back and forth on the branch.

My playhouse in the back yard had small furniture some of which I still own -- a cupboard, an ice cream table and chairs and a doll bed. There was also a small rocker and end table. My grandfather planted a rose bush for me on an arbor next to the door and the aroma was delightful.

The play house is still behind the house with the present owners but it sadly looks its age.

Winter was sledding time on the neighbor's hill across the street -- slowly trudging up the hill for the thrill of riding down head first. I don't know how I escaped hitting the tree at the end. It would slowly get so cold that I remember dragging my sled home --double mittens, hat as well as snow pants, soaking wet, and feet in shoe rubbers feeling like ice cubes. Then it was strip time in the garage and a lovely hot bath.

In fifth grade I got a regular bicycle. We had already worn out a sidewalk bike which was a small version with no brakes so, fortunately, it was not allowed on the street. You stopped by wearing out the soles of your shoes. I remember decorating the new bike with crepe paper to ride in the town parades.

Summer could be boring sometimes. I checked out library books in the tiny town library. They provided a story hour on Saturday mornings.

Paper dolls were my passion. I could spend hours cutting out the dolls and clothes and arranging them for their activities. I played with regular dolls, too, dressing and undressing them and carrying them around for a longer time than most of the girls my age.

But one usually had friends in the neighborhood who were available to play games. Mary Phil was a dear friend who lived a block west. She was younger than me but we spent many hours playing monopoly on warm summer afternoons. We would play at her house and when it was time to go home, we didn't need to put the game away, as I would have had to do at home. Her mother let it stay on the dining room floor so we could start back up the next day where we had left off.

We also played dress up in her garage with any other children who magically appeared. The clothes were holdovers from her mother's club that had rummage sales as a money maker. I question the condition those clothes were in for resale.

There were many other children in the neighborhood. Scott lived across the alley and Phil lived down the block. Some would live there for a year or so and then move away. I always thought it would be fun to move and we never did. I had my share of that in later years.

Our house was well located for school. I walked three blocks north for six years of grade school and about four blocks northwest for six years of junior-senior high. I bicycled for some of that time but usually walked because there were friends to walk with. Occasionally, in bad weather, Mother would drive us.

The playground behind the school building was divided into two sections -- younger children on the south side and older ones on the north. We had an hour and a half to walk home for lunch and return for the afternoon. In addition to the morning and afternoon recesses from studies, we had play time when we first got to school. But when the bell rang we needed to obediently line up to form a line with our classmates until our teacher led us into the building.

In the summer there were playground activities provided for children of all ages on that same school playground.

Were we deprived because television hadn't been invented? I think not. The neighborhood provided a safe, secure, comfortable, active environment where we could exercise our bodies and our minds.

LIVING IN THE THIRTIES

"Creamed chipped beef on white toast. Ugh!"

"But you have carrots that you like -- with lots of butter. And the chocolate pudding is cooling on the counter."

I would eat the carrots and slowly pick at the beef long enough that I could then eat the delicious pudding.

Mother did make some things I really liked. But she was terrible with eggs -- either fried to a crisp or boiled runny. Vegetable soup, chicken noodle soup, ham and soup beans were favorites. These were depression dishes and only required small amounts of beef, chicken or ham. Fried mush, fried chicken, fried fish, white bread, gobs of butter, lard, and real whipped cream on desserts. The word cholesterol was unknown and a balanced diet was having enough to eat. Mother had learned something about nutrition in nursing school and we had plenty of vegetables and fruit. But vegetables were either peeled or scraped and then boiled with further nutrition drained off.

We had fried fish whenever one of Daddy's friends would bring us lake fish from their family vacation trip. The fish were almost all bones and were eaten with white bread to absorb any bones that were accidentally swallowed. The best fish meal for me was scalloped canned salmon and baked potatoes swimming in butter. Dessert was often pudding -- tapioca, rice, or chocolate. Jell-O was a new item -- cherry, orange, lemon, lime. Sugar needed to be added with the hot water. Mother had learned how to make a jelly roll and angel food cake with powdered sugar frosting when she was a girl, and they were her specialties.

We had never heard of pizza or spaghetti. Rice was for pudding. In later years my parents enjoyed a Chinese restaurant and Mother attempted Chinese food with some success.

On Thanksgiving we had a big turkey dinner in the dining room which included mashed potatoes, dressing, and cranberry sauce. Daddy liked to take the turkey wish bone and hang it on the dining room chandelier to dry. After there were several hanging there they disappeared -- not Mother's idea of décor. But it was novel and fun.

In those days it was dinner at noon and supper at night. I didn't hear the word lunch until I had gone away to school.

Fast food meant sitting on a stool at the counter of a regular restaurant. We had never even heard the word "drive-thru" or "drive-in." Most people ate all meals at home sitting around the kitchen table.

The house on Third Street was new and modern for its time as a small modest dwelling. Mother cooked on a coal oil stove at first and then got a new gas stove to light with matches. We had an ice box and the ice man came once or twice a week to deliver ice and place it in the box. Mother would put the card in the window to indicate how much ice she needed with the correct number on top facing up. There was another number at the bottom upside down and one on each side.

Mother

The ice man used a pick to break off the ice and kept the supply covered with canvas. Boys would follow the truck to savor any chips that might fall to the ground.

Ice for cold drinks was chipped off the block in the ice box with an ice pick. We had a chipper at the store which would chip off many small chunks with one thrust.

When we did get a more modern refrigerator, ice would accumulate and need to be defrosted weekly. But it did have an ice cube tray which was quite a treat.

We had an electric washer in the basement which would churn the clothes clean at a regular speed. Then the electric wringer on the side would extract the water. Clothes were hung outside on the clothes line in desirable weather and on a line strung across the basement at other times.

Our basement had a concrete floor and I learned to roller skate when there were no clothes hanging.

After the clothes and other washed items had dried, they were dampened, rolled, and placed in an oilcloth lined bushel basket with the sheets on top ready to be ironed the next day. If they stayed there too long they would mildew. Everything was ironed because permanent press had not been invented.

The basement had a double sink next to the washer to use for hand wash items and to starch some things before they were dried. There was also a fruit cellar for food storage and a coal bin for the large furnace which dominated the downstairs.

The coal truck delivered coal and two men shoveled it into a small trap door to the basement room which faced the driveway. It was noisy rolling down the chute. In winter the fire was kept burning constantly but it would die down in the night after being banked with ashes so it wouldn't go out entirely. The house was always cold in the mornings and I often dressed on the furnace registers.

Everyone burned coal for heat, but some gradually modernized to oil furnaces. Not my parents, incidentally. Chimneys spurted black smoke from every house as I walked to school in the winter. The beautiful white snow would be speckled with black dots from all the coal furnaces. The walls in our house showed a dusting of dirt in the spring and Mother had each room cleaned with a product that is probably no longer available. And before we had wall to wall carpeting covering the hard wood floors, the rugs must be removed and aired and cleaned outside.

The yard was mowed with a push mower and trimmed with big scissors. Nothing mechanical was available for home use and during the war no tools could be replaced. In those hard years metal was definitely not for civilian use.

Mother always made a detailed grocery list and we would stand at the counter while a clerk hurriedly walked around the store accumulating the items and placing them on the counter. Only basic items were available. There were no frozen foods or mixes of any kind and meat needed to be purchased at a meat market. Then the total was added up on the cash register and Mother paid in cash. Credit cards were unknown. Of course, Mother might have plucked a few bananas off the huge bunch hanging from the ceiling by the doorway on our way into the store to add to her purchases.

But we didn't need to leave the house to buy groceries. Mother could sit in the kitchen chair by the wall telephone and read off her grocery list. Then a boy from the grocery store would deliver the items in a box at our back door and then place them on the kitchen table. He would even carry change in a money pouch in case Mother didn't have the right amount.

Some people would charge their groceries or "run a tab" at the store. My parents prided themselves that they always paid cash. Daddy said that a charge was like "paying for a dead horse."

Milk was placed on our doorstep in the early morning hours. We had a standard order. The milk would separate with the cream on top which could be removed for desserts. In the winter the milk would freeze and rise to the top of the glass bottle in an ice cap.

The mailman walked his route with a large leather bag over his shoulders. The mail was placed in a mailbox located on the wall next to the front door. The mail consisted of letters with a three cent stamp and post cards with a one cent stamp or a penny card purchased at the post office. Picture post cards sent from a vacation spot were familiar.

Our telephone was always on the wall in the kitchen with a chair next to it and the phone book hanging from a hook on the wall. To make a call one would pick up the cone shaped receiver off the hook on the telephone box and hear the operator say, "Number, please." Then she would connect to whatever number you requested unless that number was busy. Then you needed to try again later. Our home number was 552. Three digits and some had one digit numbers. Calling long distance required the same procedure. Telephone operators had the reputation of knowing all the business in town because when they weren't busy they were able to listen in on people's conversations.

Doctors made house calls. Dr. Bunker carried a black bag with an assortment of bottles that looked really interesting. She would count out some pills for me and write down directions. Again it was a pay as you go --health insurance unknown.

For serious illnesses one needed to go to Wabash or Fort Wayne for hospital care. I had my tonsils taken out in Fort Wayne but fortunately had no other childhood hospital visit. We were inoculated for diphtheria and smallpox but none were available for measles and chicken pox and mumps.

```
              C. EUGENE COOK, M. D.
                      112 N. MARKET
     OFFICE HOURS:  9 TO 11:30 A. M., 1 TO 4 AND 7 TO 8 P. M.
                       PHONE 721

   ATIENT'S NAME   Jane Ann Marks

       ADDRESS

                       DATE
   ℞

           Vaccinated for Smallpox
           April 14, 1942




   JLL  NAME   C. Eugene Cook,          M. D.
                  REG. NO. 5035  C. Y.
```

So we all suffered through those illnesses as they rotated through the school. I remember one year when half the class was home sick. We just expected to endure those illnesses as part of growing up. Polio was the absolute terror!

For entertainment and for current news there was the radio. Our newspaper was published twice a week so we could be informed of town events. The two movie theaters did a thriving business advertising that they were "cool inside" in the summer because electric fans and opening windows were the only ways to keep cool on hot summer days every place else. With no television most of us enjoyed a movie almost every week and the movies were all censored and "clean."

We felt we were living a good comfortable life in small town USA. And in many ways we were. No one talked of a possible war that would change our lives forever. We had modern conveniences far better than the previous generation. And we had a kind caring community where children could walk to each other's houses at night and many people didn't even lock their doors. How could anything change?

DAYS AT TOMMY R

"You don't mean that little thing starts school next year?"

"She'll be six in September."

"But she's so small and shy. Too bad they don't have kindergarten here like they have started in some of the city schools."

"Jean will do just fine. She's very smart."

Mother walked me to school that first sunshiny fall day accompanied by my barely two year old brother toddling along.

"Now remember where we're walking because you'll need to return home for lunch the same way."

So the shy little thing started school and remained that shy little thing for the first two years of school. I was deathly afraid of my teacher. But I learned and had a good foundation for the rest of my life.

We learned to read with a primer and a workbook and a wall chart which duplicated the individual materials. We studied phonics and sight words and putting it all into sentences with meaning. We filled in pages of a math workbook. We had a handwriting teacher who appeared once or twice a week and the pencil was held exactly right. She wrote letters in chalk on the blackboard but I was never able to duplicate her perfect writing, even after tracing the letters in my handwriting workbook. We would later use pens dipped into an ink jar. Fountain pens were a later invention.

The art teacher also made the rounds a couple times a week and her materials were very carefully counted out. There was no waste in those depression times.

Thomas Marshall School was strategically located between the college and down town. So we often had student teachers who needed practice hours in the school room. At that time only two years of college were required to teach. I felt they had an unending supply of aspiring teachers and as soon as one had improved, there was another to take the place. Mother considered this an advantage because the regular teacher had had additional training to qualify for the supervising job. I disagreed. And, in addition, many of my classmates were children of college professors so I felt those students had an unfair advantage.

But the shy little thing just slumped in her seat and learned.

Mother had two rules on walking to school. This was in addition to watching for traffic and not getting lost. One I did not follow and one I did.

My friend, Mary Emma, persuaded me to come home with her after school so we could play awhile and have a good time. I told her I wasn't supposed to do that. I needed to walk straight home. She was very persuasive and I agreed. But after I had been at her house just a short time her mother said, "Jean, does your mother know where you are?"

I ducked my head and nodded a no. She called my distraught mother and I didn't do that again.

I was more cautious in following the rules before my next possible indiscretion. As I was walking to school, a car slowly stopped next to me and a man called out the open driver's window.

"Let me give you a ride to school."

"My mother told me I'm not supposed to ride with anyone."

"She means strangers. But I'm Lowell's father and he's in your class and he's sitting right here." He motioned toward the passenger seat.

"No, I can't."

He asked me again and then drove on.

I didn't know then but he was probably the most famous person I have ever known. He was Andrew Cordier who became assistant to the secretary general of the new United Nations. But I followed the rules and did not accept a ride to school.

For second grade ten of us stayed in the first grade room with the same strict teacher. I was so disappointed because I wanted to be in Miss Wright's room. She taught all of third grade and half of second. I realize now that it was a complement to be held back because we were ability grouped and the best students were retained in the first grade room. They would then be better able to do seat work while the teacher spent more time with her inexperienced first graders who, of course, had had no kindergarten opportunities.

Then I had Miss Wright for third grade and Miss Brane for fourth and fifth grades. Lady teachers were always single and when they married they were supposed to stay at home and be housewives.

School days were short with an hour and a half break for lunch so that we could walk home and back for the afternoon session. But we did work hard. I remember memorizing poetry, memorizing basic math facts, memorizing history facts and dates. I often used the walking time to do this and would carry a paper of requirements in my pocket. I think that experience was useful in college years when I studied for serious examinations.

Our report cards also included our weight so we would line up for this procedure. Pat, Mary, and I were the shortest and lightest in the class and we would try to stand in line together and then compare statistics. We each hoped that we would be the one to finally grow.

There were just ten students in my fifth grade class. I enjoyed Miss Brane as a friend and teacher. How ironic that fifth and sixth grades were my favorite school years and that many years later I would be teaching at that level.

Mr. Burr was another favorite teacher. In addition to teaching half of fifth grade and all of sixth, he was the school principal. With all that responsibility he always seemed happy in his job. He supervised the game of "black man" on the playground. This would never be played in these racially conscious times. But we lived in an all white community and didn't even realize the significance of the name. To play the game, we would run back and forth in an area of the playground trying not to be captured and put on the sidelines. Louis broke his collarbone playing and he lay on the ground until the teacher could go in the school and call his parents to take him to their doctor. He wore his arm in a sling for a long time.

We did some serious crafts in sixth grade and I now have the wooden pig cutting board that I carefully sawed out and painted as a gift for my mother.

All classes did field trips but they were not by bus. We would walk in procession behind the teacher with the student teacher at the end. This was usually to a program of some kind at the high school where we could sit in the balcony and then walk back to school the same way. At times we went to special events at the college and once to the college library.

We did little folk dance performances of our own. We always observed Armistice Day on November 11 by silence for one minute and we knew the meaning of that day. Patriotism was very important and we saluted the flag and knew the rules of the flag.

We celebrated holidays with art work and songs in music classes with a special music teacher. We made and exchanged Valentines and I learned the words to all the major Christmas songs. Some of us brought cookies to class for our birthdays.

In music class we not only sang but played in a rhythm band. I always hoped that I could be promoted from tapping sticks together to the beat of the piano to tapping triangles which had a more melodic sound. But I never was. For most of the children recess was an important part of the day. But there were few games that I really enjoyed, either on the playground or in an empty classroom which we sometimes used for activities. This was probably because I was never good at the games and didn't care whether we won or lost. So, I was always last chosen for team play. This carried into Phys. Ed. in high school.

Throughout my school years girls wore dresses and the teachers were unmarried. In elementary school I remember wearing little cotton dresses that tied in the back. They had been starched and ironed at home. Of course there were no zippers and I don't even remember snaps. In the winter we wore heavy snow pants and boots that with difficulty, fit over our natural leather shoes. It was even more difficult to remove the boots. We had hats, and scarves and mittens because we walked to school.

In high school, during the war, we wore skirts and sweaters with saddle shoes or penny loafers with a penny tucked in top of each shoe. Unrationed shoes looked better than they felt, but we didn't want to wear saddle shoes to school dances.

When I was in college after the war, fashions changed. Fabric was available for full skirts. Zippers were invented but were somewhat unreliable. It was necessary to also buy a repair kit for the zipper, but sometimes it didn't work.

The Thomas R. Marshall School building still stands but not as a school. It had been named for a vice president of the United States who was born in the town and it was a modern progressive edifice for its time.

"Tommy R?" That was a show off nickname the popular students used, thinking that the name made them sound really important.

Many, many honest successful people began their education in that school and without any modern technology. This stands as a tribute to four teachers who worked tirelessly; with few basic materials and low depression era salaries. But those teachers did have unending parental support and few discipline problems. My guess is that the majority of the students became college educated after a solid basic elementary education.

DOWN A ROCKY ROAD

My grandfather's death marked a turning point in the road.

James B. (JB) Marks, my grandfather 1876-1938

Soon after, my brother acquired a serious illness and I was moved to my grandmother's house. This was the beginning of seventh grade with a new school, students added from the other grade school, a different class schedule with a different teacher for each class, a locker with a lock, and a move to a different room when the bell rang. In the midst of all this, I had a different route to walk to a different school, and from my grandmother's house.

I wore only my old brown skirt and sweater wardrobe because no one considered new school clothes for a new school year and I felt like a misplaced orphan. My grades dropped drastically and no one seemed to even care.

My grandmother was good to me all my life, but she was in mourning for my grandfather so it was a hard time for her. She never enjoyed cooking and I don't know what we ate, but I do remember thinking that the food had been better at home. But this was how it was to be.

Grandma's sister's sister-in-law stayed with us part of the time. These were days when a family member left alone, for whatever reason, lived in their different family's homes on a rotating basis. Government help came only when the person was in need and had no family and then they were moved to the county home. Residents there did work to keep things going with a big house, animals, and a garden. There were paid supervisors. They would live there for the final days of their lives.

Lizzy was pleasant and she and Grandma had fun dressing my two antique dolls who had never had clothes. The dolls are lovely to this day.

When I returned home, I had been gone for so long that I felt like an outcast there, too.

This was the time that Mother had her opportunity to work at the store. My grandfather had taught in a one room school and he declared that Mother needed to stay home and take care of her children. But after his death she had her chance. Daddy was probably overwhelmed doing his father's previous work along with his own and grieving the father he had admired and followed all of his life. So he probably did not object to Mother's help no matter how inexperienced she was.

Mother and Daddy at the Store

This was the time that Mother started having some help at home with a cleaning woman, an ironing lady, a yard man, and baby sitters. These were all on a part time basis. Mother liked to work at the store but she didn't want to give up her clean and neat house and yard. So there were basically strangers coming to the house to do various tasks. This was a time when we ate some of our meals in restaurants because Mother said she didn't have enough time to cook.

I spent most of my days in isolation, reading in my room. The whole world turned into a rocky road and at the time there seemed no way out.

UP UP AND AWAY

Sitting in a car on a country road by a farm field, I had my first experience with airplanes. John Henry Wright had built a runway on one of the fields at his family's farm so he could take off and land his small airplane. All would gaze in amazement as this farm boy performed. My parents enjoyed many a pleasant Sunday afternoon watching this free show. John Henry was later killed in WWII.

One of my father's friends, an attorney in town, had his own plane and made frequent trips for business and for pleasure. My first plane ride was with him in the small two-seater. I was thrilled but remember thinking that it didn't really last very long.

In later years, as a special treat, when I was in school in Bloomington, he gave me a ride to school in his airplane. Then, also, I didn't think it lasted long, remembering the weary car ride making the same trip on the two lane roads. Mr. Brooks and his wife's brother were killed in a small plane crash in California in later years.

After I had graduated from college, a girl friend approached me with the idea of becoming airline stewardesses, not flight attendants as they are now known. She had the application forms and all the information. In those days the requirements for the job were very strict -- height, weight, age, education, marital status. We both met the requirements. I don't know whether she was able to follow through on the idea but I had STRONG resistance from my parents. They said that there was NO WAY that I could even consider this idea!

"I couldn't sleep at night thinking you might be going down in an airline crash!"

"We've spent money on your education but not to do this."

So being the obedient child I had been reared to be, I reneged.

As a consolation prize, I was given a trip to Denver on a commercial airline to visit my college girlfriend who was working there on summer vacation. In those days, of course, it was hat, gloves, hose, heels, purse, and a suitcase that was carried, not wheeled.

Since then I have traveled half way around the world twice and overseas and domestic many times. Everything is casual and open. I have stood in a check-in line minus shoes, purse, and carry-on bag wondering what I would do if they didn't reappear. I have eaten lovely gourmet meals on foreign flights and my own packet of trail mix from home on domestic trips. I have sat on hard benches trying to stay awake to change planes. And, I have listened to people talk to each other in many foreign languages in every kind of airport from super efficient Singapore to the mess at LAX.

I still marvel, as I did as a child sitting by that corn field, "How can that big heavy thing go up in the air?"

A GHOST IN THE HOUSE

"Ooooh, I hear the ghost. I think it's coming up the stairs."

"Don't worry. She's a friendly ghost. I think she lived in this room and comes back to visit."

We lay in the big bed in the big guest room in the hundred year old house as we had so many nights. It was warm and cozy under the blankets and quilts even though the coal furnace would die down in the night.

These were the innocent years before we became teenagers and the War would change our lives forever. It was before we saw our mothers working and older boys we knew joining the services and dying. Before we knew rationing and shortages and star flags in windows.

How often would we stop in your house and I can still smell the pot of soup on the stove -- bean soup, vegetable soup, potato soup with rivelets. Your mother would ladle out a bowl for each of us with soda crackers and milk.

How often would we play table games or piano duets for the evening and when time flew by your mother would call my mother, "Louise, the girls are still playing the piano and Jean can just spend the night."

Then we would retire to the ghost room because you and your sister shared another with twin beds and little upholstered rocking chairs that I loved.

We walked to school and did outside fun things, too. In our small Indiana town we roller skated, sledded, bicycled, and played hopscotch. We knew each other's families including grandparents. We went to Sunday School together.

In wartime high school we sang, partied, danced, laughed, and tried to forget a country at war.

In college years we compared notes on our different schools and reunited with high school friends.

I took baby pictures of your Kathy who is now a grandmother. You visited me in the hospital with my Loraine who is now also a grandmother. We took trips together and visited in each other's homes.

Even though we live in different states, we still visit our small town cemetery together and discuss the people who are buried there that we knew.

Is it possible that a friendship would endure over seventy-five years. But its closeness began in that ghostly guest room. Maybe our ghosts now live in that room and other young girls are giggling and whispering there completely unaware of what their future will bring.

PARK BEGINNINGS

"Shush. It's Billy Sunday." I squirmed on my grandfather's lap as we sat next to my grandmother in the large tent revival meeting at Winona Lake. My grandfather's father and brother had both been ministers in the Church of Christ denomination so he was, of course, interested in what the famous evangelist had to say. I would lean back and sleep through the long dramatic sermon because I was too young to understand what was going on.

I often went places with my father's parents, sitting between them in their car. I was their only grandchild in those days. Sunday was a day off from work. Almost all businesses were closed all day. Daddy worked a few hours in the morning to fill prescriptions as needed. But my grandparents often went places and took me along. I had been taught to be the obedient little child who was "seen and not heard."

My grandparents often took me to visit Grandpa's parents who lived in a log cabin house near North Webster, where they are now buried. I remember my great grandmother as being a large woman who wanted me to sit on her lap but I would hover near my grandfather instead.

Jonas Warvel lived in the house behind my grandparents' house and he and my grandfather were good friends as well as neighbors. The Warvels had a small lily pond in their back yard with gold fish swimming around. With the lilies blooming and the fish swimming, it was a beautiful sight. The two couples would sit in lawn chairs overlooking this attraction and I would sometimes be included.

Mr. Warvel had a large plot of land at the edge of town next to his friend, Mr. Peabody's, acreage. His hobby was unusual birds and he kept them in little pens on one side of the property. Grandpa would often take me with them when they went to care for the birds. The whole space was like a little nature park and the peacocks spreading their wings made quite an impression on a young child. This area was later to become the town park, Warvel Park.

Bob McNear was older than me but he lived just a block down the street and I often saw him riding his bicycle. After he was killed in the War, I learned that he had been an honor student and an Eagle Scout. He had been his parents' only child and they willed money to the town for a scout cabin to be built at the park. It stands on about the same location as the bird pens had been located. The McNear's are pictured in the cabin but I feel their son should have been included since his scouting success was undoubtedly the reason for their generosity.

My grandparents' house had a lovely screened front porch with wicker furniture and a swing at one end. It was their main living area in the summer and Grandpa would stuff his newspapers in the side of the cushion of his wicker chair when he had finished reading them.

Grandma would sit in the swing and do needle work. I became interested in all kinds of sewing from watching two grandmothers as I was growing up.

My father's mother had been raised on a farm in Kosciusko County and she talked about riding a "hack" or bus to school. Country schools then were available only through eighth grade and to further an education a child needed to live in town, possibly with relatives. Grandma had taken piano lessons and she enjoyed playing her piano.

My grandparents always had a small garden at the back of their property and a bower of roses along one side of the garage.

After Grandpa died I would go places with Grandma -- to swim at Long Lake, to visit relatives, and to shopping trips in Fort Wayne. I remember her being a very unsafe driver and I don't know why my parents allowed me to go. I guess they were just busy with the business so didn't give it any concern.

Warvel Park now has a picnic area, a playground, an indoor pool, and the scout cabin, which is also used for other community activities. I walk there and think about the time that it was primitive nature with the bird displays and Mr. Warvel pointing out the different species when I only enjoyed the peacocks with their spreading wings.

FIRE! FIRE!

"Get your clothes on fast!! The down town's on fire. We need to get down there right away!" It was the middle of a cold February night and I urged my teenaged self to dress and get into the car. We could see the smoke the few blocks from home and after we had parked and walked there were red and yellow flames flying into the sky from the center of the south side of Main Street. Crowds had already arrived, many with coats obviously thrown over their night clothes. With our little ancient fire truck and volunteer firemen, the complete destruction of the whole town seemed inevitable.

Owners and employees of the businesses at the ends of the block were carrying their records and as much of their valuable merchandise and equipment as they could to a safe place. Bank records were transported to the hardware store across the street.

On the north side of the street employees were busy hosing water on the roofs of the buildings because fiery embers were raining down with the potential of spreading the fire across the street. The wind must have been from the south.

Of course I looked for high school friends and we enjoyed the excitement in the middle of the night. Lots to talk about the next day at school.

Fire trucks from two neighboring towns helped extinguish the blaze. However, the interior of one building was completely destroyed and the two on either side badly damaged.

The previous week one of my friends had proudly shown me the upstairs apartment she and her parents were occupying after her father had sold their farm. I remember thinking it was really neat to look down on Main Street from their living room. But their apartment was at the top of the building that was destroyed. She and her parents escaped in the middle of the night down the back outside stairway but lost all their possessions.

Descriptions of the building in the newspaper indicate a labyrinth of dead end stairways, connections of buildings by their walls, basement dungeons. The fact that the fire occurred at night may have saved the lives of those who bowled in the basement bowling alley, played pool in the pool hall, attended club meetings, or shopped in the stores.

No cause was reported. The first indication of fire was from a fellow attending the "picture show" across the street who saw flames coming out of the sidewalk grate.

The burned buildings were all replaced and repaired as time went on. Only a plaque on the wall of the brick building that completely burned is a grim reminder of the night the town almost burned down.

ALWAYS ON SUNDAY

The small town Methodist Church baptized me as an infant with my proud parents and my father's parents looking on. I don't remember that but I do remember being on the Cradle Roll in the nursery and our Sunday activity. We sat around a low table level sand box and played with various kitchen items in the sand.

I would often sit with my grandmother in church and she would entertain me with various items from her purse including "Sen Sen" which was a strange tasting breath saver of the times. I felt proud when I could read the responsive reading of Biblical scripture even though I didn't often understand the words of the King James translation of the Bible.

Many kind and faithful teachers worked hard, in those difficult depression times, instilling rules for proper Christian behavior for Sunday after Sunday in the small Sunday School classrooms which were divided by curtains in the large room. I remember hearing about Moses floating down river in a basket and it didn't seem plausible to me. We had many other stories including the friendship of David and Jonathan and, of course, the baby Jesus, born in a manger which was pictured as a wooden trough. I learned later that the mangers were actually stone in those days. But forget the details. We were taught right from wrong behavior and it made a difference in all of our lives.

In later elementary our teacher was a dairy farmer who with his wife and daughter lived outside town. He had a class party for us at his farm which included a dinner and a farm tour. But I have never forgotten his teaching us how to find books in the Bible and to find specific verses in the Bible. Then we would read those verses even though it was difficult for children to understand the King James translation.

Easter was always a special occasion at church because it meant wearing a new spring outfit complete with hat, gloves, handkerchief and purse. Often it was too cold for the spring clothes but we didn't really want to resort to wearing a winter coat.

And for Christmas parties at the church there was always singing songs of the season and a Christmas story and little bags of hard candy handed out by Santa in a make shift outfit. I never really liked the hard candy but just seeing it today reminds me of the big gatherings and other activities that were held in that big room.

Churches in town provided "penny suppers" on some evenings. These were depression times and parishioners could provide delicious food to be served at one cent a serving as a money making project. We would see people we knew in all the churches.

During this time Mother was president of the Ladies Aid organization at church. Because married ladies were housewives, this was a social time as well as a service to support missionaries. The ladies had little containers to hold their coin offerings for each day. I remember Mother playing "catch up" on the day that they turned them in. Mother also sang in the town's Mother's Chorus and portrayed the Biblical Ruth at the Eastern Star Lodge.

Our high school Sunday School teacher was my favorite teacher in school. He taught three levels of high school English and then worked with us again on Sunday. And we had Methodist Youth Fellowship which I attended occasionally but it wasn't particularly memorable.

Of my high school class of just thirty-five students, four were "Preacher's Kids." And two of them sang in our small senior choir. We memorized religious music and sang in all of the protestant churches in town. There were no Catholics and no blacks. The few Jews went to a neighboring synagogue. I really enjoyed singing in the choir. I would recognize many of the parishioners in the congregations because I worked at the soda fountain after school, on Saturdays, and also many evenings. So I would prepare their ice cream treat on Saturday night and then sing for them at church on Sunday morning.

The little Methodist Church of my youth still partially stands but as an office building with only the main stained glass windows as a reminder of the thriving congregation which once met and worshiped there.

My religious life continued at Stephens College. The school had been organized as a church affiliated finishing school for young ladies in the area. We were required to attend the church of our choice on Sunday and the Burrell vesper service on Wednesday evening. For attendance we would collect our own name card in the dormitory as we left the building and then hand it to the person collecting at the door of the religious service. I enjoyed visiting churches of every denomination on Sundays including the Catholic Church whose service was entirely foreign to me. This was probably a continuation of my high school music performances. The Wednesday night service was really a pleasant respite from study. The auditorium was darkly lit and music by various music students and the inspirational talk made a pleasant pause in the school week. Having prayer at activities seemed a natural thing to do.

My good friend, Marilyn, could often persuade me to walk with her to Sunday services at the Methodist Church near downtown Bloomington, Indiana while we were attending Indiana University. Her mother was organist at her hometown church, her grandfather had been a minister, and she continued the practice of regular church attendance that she had always known. Often on Sunday evening, since there was no dormitory food, one of the girls with a car would take a bunch of us to a cheap restaurant at the edge of town. On one memorable occasion we almost set the place on fire. As we were leaving, one of the girls casually laid her paper napkin close to the decorative lit candle. We all hurriedly poured water from our glasses on the ever increasing flame, put out the fire, and made a hurried exit.

An architecturally beautiful Methodist Church still occupies a spot a block from the historic square in Marshall, Missouri. My three older children were all baptized in that church as infants. Later, as visitors, we would all attend the church service, Sunday School, and any church suppers which were given while we were there. I can still remember the delicious food and the kind friendly people. I cherish their cookbook.

The old classic Methodist Church in Wabash, Indiana sits next to the railroad tracks so one can hear trains rattling by at various times. It was here that my youngest child was baptized as a toddler with no fanfare or family dinner following the ceremony.

The Methodist Church in Goshen, Indiana also has the classic stone exterior with steps leading up from the outside and twin stairways traveling up on either side of the interior hallway to the sanctuary. When we joined that church we were a family and church activities and services were family oriented. I joined the Nursery Guild for mothers with young children. Most of my friends there throughout the years had been members of that group. We attended all church services and activities while the children were growing up and they attended Methodist Youth Fellowship and formally joined the church. In later years, the church had Wednesday night suppers with Bible study. I went with the church group on their trip to Israel which was a really memorable experience.

However, as time went on, even after working in the Women's Society, I did not feel comfortable in that church. It was basically family oriented and activities there followed that direction and did not meet my needs. It became hard to maintain interest and I gradually drifted away.

When I moved to Indianapolis one of the first people to greet me in the neighborhood was the choir director of St. Luke's Methodist Church. He persuaded me to attend some of their many activities. A year later I transferred my Goshen membership of forty years and also joined the choir. I have many pleasant memories of being a choir member. I enjoyed the church Christmas programs, the choir parties, and the trips. We went by bus to St. Louis and sang in the huge cathedral there and had a tour of the facility. We went to Chicago and sang in the skyscraper church where I had attended as a tourist years before. When my eyes became a problem I slowly lost interest.

The Church of God, recommended by friends of my daughter, Linda, has become my church now, although the Methodist denomination remains ingrained in me. One great grandfather donated land for a church in Kosciusko County. Another great grandfather and my grandfather's brother were both ministers. But I especially enjoy the open friendliness of the Church of God and the serious Bible teaching.

So I've come a long way from wearing that long white baptismal gown. But on that way I've known many, many lovely Christian people who have met my needs at various stages of my life.

FIELD TRIP DISASTER

Near the end of my third grade year at Thomas Marshall School a tragedy occurred that I have never forgotten. On a beautiful spring day in May, at the end of the school year, what could be more pleasant for students than a walk to a park for an outing and picnic. The setting was idyllic with a large grassy area by the Eel River and with a waterfall rambling over a dam. The young teacher and her student teacher were preparing the picnic while the children played nearby.

Suddenly there was a shattering of loud screams! One of the girls had fallen from the top of the concrete dam into the racing water below!

Nearby a young fellow had been fishing with a friend and three of his four small sons. He hastened to help by jumping into the river and grabbing the girl by her hair. Sadly they were both pulled under in the tow. Rescuers pulled the man's body from the water within a few hours but they were unable to find the body of the girl.

This was a Saturday and the bi-weekly newspaper would not publish the news until Monday. But in a small town news travels fast. What I didn't hear by eavesdropping I learned at school the next Monday morning.

Boats and grappling hooks had been used to recover the man's body. Now more boats were sent out in an attempt to find the girl. Three of those boats capsized in the swollen river water. Fences and nets were strung across at bridges to catch the body if it floated downstream.

As a third grader in lower elementary I barely knew the girl. She was one of the older students with a room upstairs and recess at a different time. And she lived in a different direction from school than I did. Nevertheless, I had horrible dreams every night. I would see the girl floating down the river and my bedroom in the house was on the side toward the river.

I heard Mother say that the family had hired a psychic who told them that the body of the girl was under the dam. The workers may have believed the psychic or have attempted the recovery as she had directed because they had no other alternatives. For whatever reason, their next attempt was to fill sand bags and pile them on the dam to lower the river. Volunteers and college students completed the task. So eight days after she drowned, Patsy Schubert's body was found caught in barbed wire under the dam and pulled to the surface.

While this was happening the family was at their church having a memorial funeral service for the little girl. The news was announced after the service that the body had been recovered and that there would be a private burial in the town cemetery the next day.

In later years I was required, as part of my teaching job, to do lengthy field trips for sixth and then fifth graders. I would always tell them a condensed story of the field trip drowning. Of course I would emphasize that students their age should be aware of dangerous situations and walking out on a slippery concrete river dam was not wise. I neglected the fact that the supervisors were two young women who were not watching these children in an unsafe place.

I would also tell students the story of one of my son's field trips when a high school student was left at a Chicago museum. He did the wise thing and went to the museum office where he was able to call home. His parents told him to wait there and if the bus didn't return for him they would drive to Chicago. After the group had stopped for dinner he was missed and they returned for him making everyone late. But, of course, the lesson was that if you get lost on a field trip, find an authority, report your problem, and wait. Don't go with a stranger!

The students all learned these lessons well and we had no serious problems. My co-teacher for most of the fifth grade trips was a young fellow who was tall and big. We planned our trips well and were experienced and organized. The students were assigned into small groups with either a teacher or parent. Those parents would have their own child with possibly a few friends and teachers had the problem children with them.

We also had a bus system that worked well. My fellow teacher always sat in the back of the bus where all the wild ones wanted to sit and there were no problems when he was there. I would sit in the front of the bus and help the driver with directions and schedule so he or she could safely watch the road. We proudly had excellent educational trips. Most of my later ones were to

Indianapolis and we would tour the Children's Museum, the Capitol Building, and Conner Prairie.

Fortunately we didn't do the trip where the student tried to run away from home but we heard about it in the teacher's room. I did have one boy whose sweater I groped any time he was off the bus because I was concerned about losing him. And we had a mother who got sick on the bus on our way to Indy and we left her at a truck stop so she could call her husband to pick her up. And at our Kokomo rest room stop where adults could have refreshments but not students, one mother bought her child a snack, too, which he could flaunt in front of his classmates. Others had their snack food from home and McDonald's for the return trip in order to save time.

I started with a sad field trip but I'll end with a happy note. The return bus ride on all the trips was always noisy. Happy excited tired children resulted in a miserable ride for the adults. As usual, on this particular one, I was counting the time and miles until we could reach the school. Suddenly word was passing from student to student and then a miraculous silence. I didn't question why because it was such a pleasant change from the loud clatter. A short distance from the school my co-teacher walked to the front of the bus, looked around at everybody and stated, "You have been quiet and have earned your reward." He proceeded to remove his hair piece and revealed his always hidden shiny bald head. The students all cheered.

SCHOOL FIRE INCIDENTS

"In case of fire, throw this in!" How often I would see this on the front page of the used text book my mother had acquired for me and then the name of an older student I barely knew. Without a book rental system and in depression times, the mothers would do a used book exchange by telephone. At school we had our required fire drills but I never had the opportunity to "throw the book in," at least not as a student. But as a teacher things changed.

"Don't say anything, but this is the real thing. The school is on fire," a fellow teacher whispered as we led our students in parallel lines down the hall to the outside exit. I had already concluded that it was miserable weather for a fire drill with a dark sky and drizzling rain. And, I had considered calling in sick that morning because my cold was worse.

With the children outside the building in their designated areas I stood shivering and questioning and then walked back to the door and looked inside. There was a little smoke and I asked another teacher, "Where's the fire?"

"In the kitchen."

Fire trucks began whizzing by and cold excited students without coats in the rainy weather jumped excitedly or huddled together for warmth.

I cheated. With aching head and runny nose I slipped back into the building to retrieve my coat and purse with my car key. When I got to my room the smoke was so thick that it was impossible to see down the hall. But I did stand at the door a minute and realize that all this would be gone.

When I returned outside, some of the teachers had taken all of the children to the playground to play running games of any kind so that they could try to get warm. They needed to wait for school bus drivers to be called.

The firemen were busy putting out the fire and did contain it in the kitchen area. According to later reports, a defective deep fat fryer had caught fire in the kitchen. Prescribed chemicals proved ineffective but the good old fire hoses saved the school from burning to the ground.

The aftermath of the fire was disbelief and survival. The smoke smell permeated the building. The kitchen was closed off but one glance in revealed a charred mess. Students were asked to carry their lunches for the remainder of the school year and we ate in the class rooms. Milk was served in paper cups in the hall and we carried it back to the rooms. Of course, we had no air conditioning or screens on the windows. No matter how careful we tried to be, flies were a terrible problem, particularly during the hot spring afternoons.

The kitchen was repaired, of course, but we all remember the big school fire.

The other time the school almost burned to the ground was at the beginning of a school day. That time it was not as exciting as the previous time but was still just as real.

There was a smell of burning when I entered the building in the morning. An adult in the building commented to me that the janitor was having trouble with one of the furnaces.

"All adults evacuate the building immediately!" sounded over the loud speaker. From the voice tone I knew that this was serious. Students had already been kept from entering the main part of the school and most were playing in the gym but were now moved outside to wait for the bus ride home.

This time I could linger a moment and wonder if, besides my coat and purse, there was anything I might want to rescue before the building was lost. I picked up a few papers I had recently typed and left.

Again, the firemen extinguished the fire and school continued on and we smelled smoke for the remainder of the school year.

We knew that in case of fire we didn't need to throw the book in because of the possibility of losing that book and everything else.

WAY UP AND DOWN UNDER

"When you can see the monument we'll be almost to Indianapolis," my mother stated.

"Look over there at the house with the iron fence painted gold at the top; it is our governor's house," added my father pointing eastward.

As we rode south down Meridian Street the Soldiers and Sailors Monument stood high as a tall building in the city. I remember gazing up and asking if we could go to the top and look out the little windows. Never did. But we might attend a movie at the Circle Theater which included a live stage show.

Seventy-five years later I did fulfill that childhood dream. A kind policeman helped me up the steps and I took a little old elevator a further distance and then climbed the narrow railed stairway to look out the dirty old windows. The view was dwarfed by tall new buildings.

Some years later the statue, Freedom, was lowered to the ground in pieces to receive much needed repairs. I witnessed her as she lay on the grass before being lifted to the top by a monster crane.

After the interior had been repaired a few years later, my daughter took me to the top of the monument again and we viewed the Indianapolis skyline and the multitude of big buildings.

I'm not much on heights but I have done some other tall towers. A college girl friend, Marilyn and I rode the numerous elevators to the top of one of the World Trade Towers in New York City.

It was a cloudy day but I'm glad to have had that experience since the twin towers no longer exist because of the 9-11 tragedy. Another highlight of New York City was the Brooklyn Bridge. The view from the bridge was spectacular. We also went to the top of the Statue of Liberty.

The Prudential Building in Chicago was a big tourist attraction at one time because the view at the top was outstanding. Later the John Hancock Building and then the Sears Tower outdid their predecessor. The views from all these buildings with the city skyline and Lake Michigan are spectacular and I was able to experience them numerous times.

The Seattle Space Needle can also claim its fame. My daughters and I ate in the revolving restaurant after walking around the top to gaze at the view.

Seattle with daughters Loraine and Linda

My desire growing up was always to see things from the top if it wasn't too high.

Hiking in Vermont with daughters Loraine and Linda

But it wasn't to go underground any lower than our basement. And there was a reason for that. As a child we took a family vacation trip to Tennessee and Kentucky where we visited Mammoth Cave.

"In a few minutes I'll be turning off my flashlight and you will experience complete darkness," stated the guide. I cringed knowing that flashlight batteries were not that reliable and wondering how we could escape in that complete darkness.

Many years later a teacher girl friend and I made a summer trip to Opryland in Nashville and we toured Mammoth Cave on the way home. I don't remember any of the fear that I felt on that previous trip. The views underground were unbelievable and the temperature is always the same. We had a very enjoyable vacation.

Growing up I remember seeing pictures of places that absolutely fascinated me. In those days I had no idea that as an adult I would actually see and walk at those places. Two were completely disappointing and one very surprising.

The Rock of Gibraltar and Diamond Head Mountain in Hawaii were disappointing because they were hollowed out shells. The Great Pyramid in Egypt was surprising because there is a room underneath and I walked down under the pyramid to this room.

CLOAK ROOM COATS

"I think this is my coat but my car keys aren't in the pocket. How will I get home?" A group of us friends were leaving a South Bend restaurant after a pleasant dinner.

Vince talked to the manager about his coat while the rest of us looked through the assortment of coats on the rack with no success.

"I'll take you home," I offered since I lived in his vicinity.

The next day the manager called him and Vince was able to retrieve his identical coat with the keys in the pocket and to drive his car home. I think Vince and the coat snatcher must have been the same size and have shopped in the same place.

Frequently in the church news my friend, Martha, would ask if anyone had mistakenly taken her new coat from the coat rack in the church. By fall she gave up and bought another new coat. Then, surprisingly, she received a phone call from a friend who would never intentionally have taken anything.

"When I got my winter clothes out of the hall closet, there hung your coat. I must have mistakenly taken it at the church last spring."

I know how embarrassed she must have felt because I did the same thing.

I had just gotten home from a meeting at the church and the phone rang. "I know we both have similar coats but I think you have the wrong one." True! A return trip solved the problem.

My friend, Sally, lost her coat in a restaurant and never retrieved it. When the business closed there were no coats remaining.

After an enjoyable dinner my friend helped me with my coat and we left to meet others for a party dance at the Elkhart Moose. Sitting in the car I reached into my pocket for my gloves. There were gloves but not my gloves.

"You'll have to turn around and go back. I'm wearing someone else's coat."

So we did and I slipped in the door and exchanged coats. The owner never realized that her coat had been worn by a stranger.

"Mother, what are you doing with those old coats in the closet taking up space?"

"Those are my cloak room coats. If I wear a good coat some place I sit on it. But if I know the coat needs to be left on a coat rack or in a cloak room, I wear one of these coats. Then if it is taken either intentionally or accidentally, no problem. And I haven't lost one of them yet.

"By the looks of those coats, that I can believe!"

A DANGEROUS JOB

"Call my husband to come and take me to a doctor!" The young art teacher held one hand against the other wrapped in her sweater. I was standing near the doorway talking to the school secretary seated at her desk.

"What seems to be the trouble?"

"I cut off my finger in the paper cutter!"

Another young teacher soon approached and said, "I have your finger here in a wet washcloth from the nurse's room. Get in my car now and I'm taking you to the hospital emergency."

Some weeks later, with the bandages removed, we all wanted to see her finger. It looked normal but she said she had lost all feeling in it. Previously, adults had had clothing cut accidentally in that cutter but this was the worst occurrence.

We had other injuries on the job. There was a teacher who, when decorating her classroom, placed a chair on a desk to achieve the preferred height. We all know what happened. She paid the price with a broken bone.

And, our old school building had some doors and locks that were not reliable.

"Help us open this door! HELP! HELP!" This sign was placed under the door into the hall but brought no response. The two teachers had become locked in the small nurse's room where they were changing clothes in preparation for the field day that afternoon. They pounded on the door, yelled, and sent more notes under the door. Only when they were missed at the outdoor competition did the principal hunt them and have the janitor remove the door.

Another time the music teacher was locked in her room on a week-end when she had returned for some materials. She thought that she might be trapped until Monday. Some boys were luckily playing on the playground and her signs and signals from the window succeeded in helping her escape.

We had fire drills and tornado drills. Students marched out of the building to practice escape from the former and sat in the hall facing inward in case of tornado. We had no thought of guns or nuclear attacks. But we did have our dangerous situations on the job.

MY OTHER HOME TOWN

"Look over there. That's the hospital where we got you." stated my father. We were driving north up Michigan Street in Plymouth, Indiana.

I would take a quick glance at the big old brick building and then look longingly across the street at Centennial Park with its spacious playground. The best equipment ever was the circular slide which would twist around and around to the bottom.

We might stop at the park another time but often we would be taking my grandparents on a Sunday afternoon drive north through South Bend and into the Notre Dame campus.

Daddy would comment, "I think everybody in South Bend is driving a Studebaker car." In those days that was the main industry. Other times we would drive to Culver to view the military academy.

As we drove out of Plymouth we would see a large old house with smaller buildings on the field in back. It was explained to me that it was a brewery and had been used as an underground railroad station by our relatives. Two Hoham brothers who escaped from prison in Germany and started a brewery at this location which was later used as an underground railroad station. No records of this exist because it was illegal to hide escaping slaves, but we are proud that our relatives were part of this noble venture.

On some Sunday afternoons I would sit in the parlor of my grandparents' house and listen to the thick records on the old wind-up Victrola. Sometimes, at my mother's insistence and my reluctance, I would begrudgingly play my latest memorized piano solo on the big upright piano.

At other times children might be dropped off at the big movie theater on the main street of Plymouth. In summer the sign boasted "Cool Inside." And in those summer days it was the only place that was. Then Daddy would often stop at the tobacco store on a side street to talk to his friends there and to get a shoe shine on one of the high chairs that lined one wall.

Sometimes Mother would visit during the week and she would shop at the meat market which she had known as a girl. Then we would visit Aunt Molly at work in the dry goods store. She was my grandfather's sister.

Plymouth was an exciting place for children in the summer. The circus would come to town on the big lot next to my grandparents' property. There was no way anyone in town could miss that.

And then there was Kiddy Day. All children would parade down the main streets dressed in costumes of various types, pulling crepe paper decorated wagons, riding tricycles, riding bicycles with paper streamers floating from the handle bars, or walking.

Everybody walked a lot in those years. My aunt would walk me to church. Often, at my request, we would walk across the foot bridge over the river, a Plymouth landmark.

I spent a lot of my childhood in Plymouth, spending a week or two at a time in the summer at my grandparents' home. I had neighborhood children as friends, particularly Elaine, who lived next door.

Holidays were special in Plymouth. On Memorial Day we would pack the car with lilacs and drive around to the various cemeteries to decorate graves of relatives I had never known. At the cemetery I learned that one widow was buried alone because her husband went on the California gold rush. He reached California, but died from overeating after starving while crossing the Rocky Mountains.

On Christmas there was always a little festive tree in the parlor and many family members were entertained at a big chicken dinner. I particularly remember my grandfather's brother, Uncle Jim, and my mother's sister, Aunt Martha. Children always ate in the kitchen, of course, and we were offered food only after it had circulated in the adult dining room. So I would eat in the kitchen with my brother and my cousins, Frances, Virginia, and John.

But everything changes with time. Centennial Park has expanded in size but the circular slide has remained, a tribute to solid construction after more than eighty years. The foot bridge has been rebuilt at the same spot. The hospital was moved to a new location on the other side of town and the land became a shopping center. No way could anyone drive through the center of the Notre Dame campus which is now much larger than the few buildings we would sightsee on pleasant Sunday afternoons. Studebaker cars now occupy a museum in South Bend.

I learned as an adult that I was not actually born in Plymouth, Indiana because the hospital was just outside the city limits in Marshall County. I still consider Plymouth my second hometown.

OUT OF THIS WORLD

"James is gone! I felt his spirit touch me as he passed by!" The loud wail resounded throughout the house. My grandmother's sister, Stella, lay ill in the downstairs bedroom and my mother hastened to help her. In another bedroom my mother's favorite cousin, James, lay dead. He had been sent home from college when he became seriously ill.

Always the obedient child I sat at the table in the farmhouse kitchen where I had been placed. Even though I was only two or three years old this incident has remained indelibly in my mind.

As a trained nurse my mother had been helping her relatives through this difficult time. I remember my grandmother insisting that I stay with her but since 'she will be no trouble' there I sat and listened to the whole scenario. Mother sometimes told this story but I vividly remember being there. Aunt Stella, though remarried with three young children, had only this one son from her first marriage and his death was a painful loss for her.

This was my first encounter with strange unexplained happenings.

As a teenager during WWII I listened in when my father's mother related this story to my mother. She said her sister-in-law had had a vision. "Helen was walking toward me hand in hand with her two boys and I asked her about William. "We're coming home but he will not be with us," she had said in the dream.

As an officer in the military, William survived the Batan Death March and then later died in prison. Helen and the two boys, who were elementary school age, endured a Japanese prison camp throughout the war. They returned just as in the vision, thin and worn but alive.

Before the war the four had vacationed in the United States and family and friends had urged Helen to stay in Indiana with the two boys. But to no avail. My father's cousin and her family returned to the Philippines.

78

During the War we had worried, prayed, and sent Care Packages to the prison camp. There was no communication with them throughout their imprisonment. We learned at their return that they had not received any of the parcels. But what a relief when they returned safely.

Who would have known that after a successful career in education, Helen is now in a retirement home, mentally competent at age 104. Dave retired from the military and then as a law professor. Bob, after a high school basketball achievement as a runner-up in the state basketball championship, retired from the military as a forensic scientist.

"It was evening and I sat crying in grief over the loss of my only child," a church friend related to me when I asked her about it. "He stood in front of me and I could almost reach out and touch him. 'I'm all right, Mother. Please don't cry. I'm fine,'. he said. I know it was he standing there and then he just faded away."

Her son had been a medical doctor who, at a young age, and at the start of his career, married with small children, had had a fatal heart attack. After all the work and financial struggle it seemed so unfair.

But then she told me that after he had appeared to her a burden had been lifted and she was better able to endure the loss.

I lost both of my parents, ten years apart, in the middle of the night in a hospital where each lay terminally ill. Although a frequent visitor I was not with either of them when they died. I was home and in a deep sleep completely exhausted. But at the exact time of each death I was instantly fully awakened. I had looked at the clock and then later become aware of what had happened. It was as though they had each given me a final goodbye.

My most vivid vision was after my daughter, Loraine, lost her month old baby. I clearly saw my grandfather, my grandmother, and my father standing, with my father holding that precious baby. They looked as they had when I was growing up, not sickly as in later years. They were all smiling and Daddy said, "We'll take care of him." Then they faded away.

I have had two dreams of people I knew growing up who have since died. I strongly visualized each person and felt a presence. It was as though they were checking on me and then leaving.

These stories have been a testament to me that Jesus returned to his disciples after his death. There are things out of this world that we cannot understand.

A TEENAGE VIEW OF WWII

In 1941 I was 15 years old and a sophomore in high school. Each day our history teacher showed us on a map how Hitler was conquering Europe. But that was far away and would not affect us. We were a small class of 35 giggly teenagers. The boys were planning how they would put a bucket of water over the classroom door and time it so the teacher would be rained on as he entered the room. It didn't work but is just one example of our carefree lives.

In one day everything changed -- December 7, 1941. Our family was in Chicago that Sunday and heard the news on the car radio returning home. My parents were very disturbed. The next day we heard our president say that this day would live on in infamy. Congress declared war on Japan and Germany.

The draft began immediately. With no choice, boys left jobs and school for the military. Some were 4F which meant they had a physical disability and others were exempt because of the work they were doing or were married with young children. Some refused military service for religious reasons and these were assigned work guarding prisons, staffing mental institutions, or other work that would release able bodied men to fight the war. Some were exempt to attend college and study ministry. Many family members were resentful of exemptions because their loved ones had no choice but to be put in harm's way.

After basic training the boys would come home on leave before being sent overseas. They would walk proudly around town in uniform, many with a cigarette hanging out of their mouth. Little did they know what lay ahead.

As time went on the downtown changed. There were fewer workers, less merchandise, and a dismal atmosphere. I remember my mother trying to solace her friends who cried openly because they were worried about their sons or had lost one. I don't remember funerals because the bodies were not returned.

A factory started up replacing one of the car dealerships making small telescope pieces. Many women who had never worked outside their homes began working the night shift. The foundry in town converted to war materials. Everyone endured rationing.

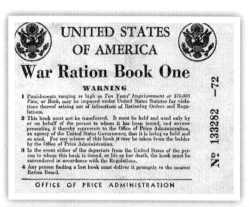

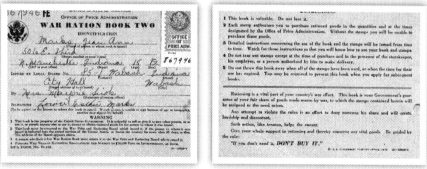

Gasoline and shoes were the two items that I noticed. Since Mother was working at the store we ate most of our meals in restaurants. But sugar and coffee rationing received many complaints. There were no spices available. Bananas hanging in a clump at the grocery entrance were no more. New cars were not produced. There were no new tires or car parts. We could buy nothing that contained metal or rubber. Sharing and repairing became a way of life. The short skirts of fashion were to conserve fabric. Victory gardens were encouraged so we would grow our own food. For a time we had black-outs with no light showing anywhere in town. Mother put blankets over the living room windows so we could have one small light on in the house.

We learned most of the war news on the radio or by word of mouth. The town newspaper was published Mondays and Thursdays only. Many times the news was very bad and other times not so bad. But the soldiers dying was a reality that was difficult to accept.

My friend, Martha, lived on the way of my short walk to high school so we would often walk together with others joining us along the way. I remember stopping for her when we went to evening activities at school. If she wasn't ready I would join her parents in the kitchen with her father sitting at the table drinking coffee and laughing with us and her mother bustling around. Martha might be finishing her cup of hot strawberry drink which was like cocoa with a marshmallow on top.

At other times I enjoyed looking through their Sear's and Ward's mail order catalogs and Martha would show me what would be her new season's wardrobe. Never in my mother's life would she order anything mail order but I would have been better dressed if she had.

I knew other boys who were drafted and killed in the war. But the loss of one of Martha's brothers affected me the most. First it was two silver stars in the window and then one was changed to gold. We were all in mourning.

In later years, at my friend Martha's funeral, her remaining brother told me that when his mother was still living he had arranged to have his brother's body returned from a European military cemetery to be buried in their family plot.

School life was not that different during the war years. It was the usual boring classes, boring textbooks, tests, and papers to write with the new fountain pens which were manually filled with ink. We carried our books and notebooks with us loose. No one knew about backpacks. I didn't find school that difficult and I just did what I was told to do. I did have classmates whose parents were college professors or other professionals and I actually felt less competition in college. It's hard to believe but the school principal and the superintendent each taught a class at the high school.

There were no sports for girls and I absolutely hated phys. ed. probably because I was the worst one in all the activities and was always chosen last for team sports. Boys had track in the spring and in winter it was Indiana basketball. Tourney time was the most exciting time of the school year. One time we actually beat Wabash to become county champions.

We had many music activities and music programs. I struggled to play my father's cornet from his Peru High School days. But we had choir that I really liked and a small senior choir which not only sang in the larger programs but also sang at all the protestant churches in town on Sundays.

The class parties were memorable -- Halloween for dress-up and Christmas for caroling and walking around town singing in the cold winter nights. I remember scavenger hunts and we were randomly put in groups to walk the town searching for items on a list to bring to the school within a time limit. This would end with refreshments at the school and some kind of prizes for winners.

All girls had Sunshine Society and boys had Hi-Y which included all the students. But the girls in my class had their own little group. We would meet in each other's homes for refreshments and conversation. Sometimes it would be for overnight. Then we could share our experiences of putting our hair in pin curls with bobby pins, the new pancake make-up, or painting our legs with the available leg paint so they would look like we were wearing the sheer silk hose that were not available.

We had dances in the gym with crepe paper hanging from the ceiling and we tried to wear the not-rationed shoes which were dressier than the rationed ones but they were like walking on cardboard.

Two movie theaters did a thriving business during this time and the skating rink was a more active diversion. Louie's Soda Shop was the teenager hangout with homemade ice cream, a very loud juke box, and Louie's friendly greeting.

We were not allowed the traditional senior class trip or a memorial year book -- no gasoline for buses or materials for books. But we were normal teenagers and tried to live our lives without constantly thinking about the war. Nevertheless, it was always with us. Boys we knew were dying overseas.

I eavesdropped on senior boys discussing what they would do militarily because they expected to be drafted. I remember one talking about Air Force airplane repair hoping that job could be an escape from death.

One class member left early and his father dramatically walked to the podium to receive his diploma. He had not been required to finish the remaining work.

I have strong memories of D-Day. It occurred days after our high school graduation. I walked down town and it was like a ghost town with complete silence. We all knew that boys from our town were dying on the beaches in Normandy.

With the War still waging I started college. Using public transportation was a nightmare. I would face huge crowds of servicemen traveling the same way. Bus and train terminals were a mass of confusion. I would often sit on my small suitcase in the aisle just to get where I was going. This proved to be good training for future years of travel.

I was 19 and in college when the war with Germany ended. Almost all of my teenage years had been during war time. During summer vacation at home the war with Japan came to an end. I remember a parade with the fire truck leading, car horns honking constantly, boys riding on car hoods, flags waving.

Underneath it all was the horrible sadness and loss, of families broken. It was easier to forget the shortages and rationing. Many of us survived to tell about it. None of the boys in my high school class were killed in the war.

Sometimes I gaze around a mall or in the grocery at the sheer quantity of merchandise and remember those war times when we had so little. But we were that "greatest generation" who survived a depression and a world war. I think there was a sharing and caring in those days that we haven't had since. It left an indelible impression on all of our lives.

THE AMISH WAY

"I suppose they drive their cars when the weather is bad," related my young daughter, Loraine, after we had moved to Goshen, Indiana when, at that time, there were many Amish buggies traveling the streets. I explained to her that because of their religion they did not drive cars, have telephones, or electricity in their homes.

Little did we know then that she would eventually marry a descendent of the Amish whose father had left the faith to join the military in World War II. Nor did we know that they would be living in a new house on land that had been farmed by his Amish ancestors and with relatives living nearby which is the Amish way. We also had no way of knowing that in a building just two blocks down the street she would be successfully practicing law.

Loraine P. Troyer, Attorney at Law

Little did I know then that I would be teaching in a country school and would occasionally have Amish children in my classroom.

I learned a lot from those children --some better behaved than others --some smarter than others --just like all the young. And most of their parents wanted the best for them. They start school at age 7 or 8 with no kindergarten because they are allowed only an eighth grade education and they can follow the law to quit at 16. Some parents want their children to attend public school, at least for the first grade or two, because the teachers are better trained and they have access to a variety of materials. Bus transportation might also be a factor.

The children are bilingual with "Pennsylvania Dutch," a form of German, spoken at home. As one mother told me, "We don't want to lose the language." I've had parents come to conferences with their horse and buggy in the school parking lot.

Unlike one religious group that we had, the Amish follow all modern medical practices. And if one is hospitalized, everyone they know visits and crowds the hallways making work difficult for the hospital staff.

A big surprise for me was a student talking about their family trip to St. Louis. I was envisioning how long it would take the poor horse to make the trip on the busy highways. But I learned that the van drivers who provide transportation to jobs, may also be hired for vacation trips. I also learned that in Amish country there are telephone booths on some of the country roads. And I even saw a horse and buggy parked at a laundromat. I talked to a young fellow not long ago who told me that he uses a computer at the library, mostly for farming information.

Amish homes are not pioneer dwellings. They are well built and have a gas tank outside to provide energy for heat, cooking, refrigeration, lights, running water, and flush toilets. Children play many outdoor games and their parents play the games with them.

Clothing is made at home for all family members. Amish women use straight pins as fasteners and wear a prayer cap under their bonnets. Married men have a beard.

Most Amish in Elkhart County are not poor. The children help with the farm work and many adults work outside the home, often in manufacturing. Just consider that if you do not pay a mortgage, keep up a car, pay for insurance and social security, buy modern conveniences or clothes, you might possibly have cash on hand. They live in a shared community and care for each other.

One of my teacher friends had been raised Amish and he would often answer my many questions. In fact, he spent some summers as a tour guide at a couple area tourist attractions. He had left the faith after eighth grade to finish high school and work his way through college in order to teach in the public schools.

Another of my teacher friends asked if I wanted to visit an Amish school. One of our best students was teaching in one and I went with her to the old fashioned one room building with a playground, out houses, and parking lot for horses and buggies.

The room was open when we were there but had a long curtain on rings to be pulled down the center. Our former student, with his eighth grade education, taught grades 5, 6, 7, and 8 on one side. A middle aged Amish lady taught 1, 2, 3, and 4 on the other.

My friend, Margaret, asked, "Is discipline a problem?"

"No, I just do like my mother. I wash their mouth out with soap and I keep a switch in the corner."

Another excellent student that we had was washing dishes in the downtown café. She might be promoted to waitress but many of us felt it was such a waste of ability

"Mother says I can invite you to church at our house on Sunday." My student had previously proudly told me that their Amish church, which was held in homes on alternate Sundays, would be at their house.

So I went. The large yard was the parking lot for horses and buggies and mine was the only car. I received a very warm welcome the minute I drove in. I had known the mother from parent conferences but everyone there was kind and friendly.

Now when I accepted the invitation nothing was mentioned about sitting on a wooden bench for three hours listening to a sermon in German (PA Dutch) given by my student's father. The children listened also and they were each given a cookie half way through. Then the boys moved the benches to the big summer kitchen where some benches conveniently converted to tables. They were placed in long rows. These benches would later be loaded into a special buggy which could transport them to the next church service location.

My hostess apologized because they fed the teenagers first and then they went outside to play games. Lunch was sandwiches and salads. I decided to forgo the community sing in the afternoon and drove home.

Through the years I've attended many church services of different denominations. But I feel it was a rare privilege to actually attend one in the Amish Christian faith.

So when you see photos of the quaint Amish standing by a buggy, keep in mind that they are not supposed to have pictures of themselves. Keep in mind, also, that some are pretty good cooks and others are not. You can't depend on that name to always mean excellence. But there are many very lovely people wearing the old fashioned clothing and doing some things the old fashioned way.

HOTEL HAPPENINGS

A large group of us tourists were sitting at picnic tables on the lawn of a hotel in Maui, Hawaii. The palm trees swayed in the warm breeze and we could view the ocean beyond the sandy beach. We all commented on the pleasant surroundings. But being there in the middle of the night had not been a part of our vacation plans.

"Screech!! All guests must evacuate the hotel immediately by stairway!! "This was constantly repeated.

I had hurriedly thrown on some clothes and made certain I had my travel purse with passport and flight ticket home.

As we sat on the lovely beach we made occasional glances at the hotel windows to see if there were flames. And in a couple hours we were allowed to return to our rooms. I never learned any details about a fire.

A previous hotel fire alarm had not been as pleasant. Since this was at a dance competition my priority was in saving my expensive dance costumes from extinction and my purse with car keys in case the hotel burned to the ground. We were eventually allowed to return to our rooms. However, the fire alarm sounded twice more before the hotel staff located the teenagers who had been enjoying their week-end excitement.

Hotel elevators may not be as reliable as we are led to believe. One elevator in a hotel in Israel stalled between floors. The maintenance staff finally got it to open on one of the floors. I immediately located the stairwell and learned to avoid foreign elevators.

You shut the hotel room door and it locks. Right? On one disastrous trip to Las Vegas this proved not to be true. Why disastrous? A South Bend teacher friend and I decided to travel to Vegas for New Year's Eve. We had previously had a happy and successful trip to Opryland in Nashville TN and wanted to repeat the fun experience. However, we each had a girl friend who insisted on joining us.

"We're all good friends and if we share a room it will be less expensive for all of us." Problems ahead. Four girls sharing a bath room was only one of them.

One girl spent her time gambling away all the money her mother had given her for the trip. One girl immediately found a boy friend and we only saw her when she loudly woke us up returning to the room in the middle of the night. One girl spent her time clinging to me as a tour guide. And the hotel room key was very unreliable. The trip did not end on a friendly note. However, I was the only one to win money. I found several tokens on the floor and cashed them in.

At one dance competition I had to take a big chance with a room lock that didn't work. Of course I complained at the desk and she said they would take care of it.

"But I'm in the dance competition and I need to dance in twenty minutes. I can't leave my things in an unlocked room!"

Can't but did. And nothing was taken.

On one trip with Linda the only motel room available was the bridal suite complete with hot tub. We turned it on and I poured in the bubble bath. We had bubbles pouring over the sides of the tub and were laughing so hard we could hardly enjoy the adventure.

Hotel breakfasts range from fresh fruit, made to order omelets and waffles, and fresh bakery items to cold sugary cereal dropping from a chute and some kind of orange colored drink. Or, no breakfast included or available.

I feel fortunate to have had all of these hotel and motel experiences and to have been able to travel all over everywhere. But I do look for the elevator inspection labels, check for stairways in case of fire, and try to open the door of a hopefully locked hotel room. Better safe than sorry!

HAPPY DANCING DAYS

"Did you know that there are tea dances in Mishawaka on Sunday afternoons?"

"What's a tea dance?"

"It isn't really tea but fruit punch and cookies and dancing in a big ball room with beautiful music and friendly people."

So the next Sunday afternoon, following her directions, I met her there in the big ballroom with beautiful music and friendly people. And, I went home with a door prize of a half hour dance lesson.

My instructor for that lesson was a pleasant young fellow who had just graduated from Notre Dame where he had been on the dance team. The lesson was enjoyable so I paid for a few more half hour lessons with him.

When he left town for a better opportunity, I eventually ended up with a contract, so I would not only have a fifty minute lesson each week but could take group lessons and attend parties on Thursday and Sunday nights. Everyone at the parties was definitely congenial and helpful and all danced with everyone there. Some wives encouraged their husbands to share their dance skills. And there were mixers with all types of music. At intermission we enjoyed refreshments and possibly a showcase with a student dancing with his or her instructor. We all applauded loudly.

Dancers worked on skill levels and passed tests to progress through the program. So we had award dance parties celebrating everyone's achievements. And we had showcase dance parties when we had worked on routines. And we had theme parties where we dressed in costume not only at Halloween but at all times of the year. I have many happy memories of those times and the friends I made and enjoyed there.

"Someone at the party told me that Brian is taking some of his students to Acapulco for a dance competition. I've been there on vacation and I would like to return and watch the dancing."

My friend, Dan O'Day, owner of the studio, hesitated, probably thinking of my meager dance skills and wondering how he could handle this and still keep my business.

Dan O'Day

"If you went you would have to dance."
I agreed because I wasn't thinking of this as a win or lose situation but just

more travel and social life. I have never been a sports competitor and didn't care who won but knew it would never be me.

Dan arranged the studio lesson schedule so that I could take enough dance lessons with his son, Brian, to compete.

Two of my friends outside the studio were excited about my going. As skilled seamstresses, experienced in doing wedding parties, they eagerly agreed to make a ball gown for me to wear.

I planned to fly to Acapulco a day early, stay at a less expensive hotel, and revisit some of the sights from my previous trip. But before I transferred to the Princess Hotel for the competition, I had my hair done by a Mexican woman in the hotel salon. She didn't speak much English but that wasn't necessary.

The Princess Hotel is lovely with a beautiful view of the Pacific Ocean, perfectly landscaped lawns, and expensively designed décor throughout. I was not disappointed watching the dancing and the ball gowns and talking to dancers from all over as long as they spoke English.

So this 'hick' amateur participated in her first dance competition in a foreign country, with a dance teacher barely known, wearing a homemade dance dress, and with hair styled by a Mexican hairdresser.

At that dance competition Brian met a beginner dance teacher from a studio in Wisconsin. They later married and the last time I saw Brian he introduced me to his three young sons.

I stayed in Acapulco for a few more days at the first hotel for a delightful cruise on the Pacific Ocean and a harrowing bus trip to Taxco. I also did some city bus trips.

A few months after we returned from Mexico, Dan asked me to go to a showcase in Indianapolis shared with a studio there. Brian had worked on a little waltz routine with me and I went, expecting this to be similar to the simple parties in Mishawaka. Big problem ahead! I had been placed last on the program! Then I could watch all the experienced dancers first. As the afternoon progressed I seriously considered hiding in the rest room. But I made it through somehow.

"Someone at the party told me that Brian is taking some of his students to the Ohio Star competition. I watch this each year on national television and I would like to go and see it live."

Dan O'Day again hesitated, "If you go to that you would need professional dance costumes."

I agreed and was presented with the forms to mail to an experienced professional seamstress. This would include measurements and photos. We made arrangements on the phone and I gulped at the price for both smooth and rhythm attire. They arrived barely in time for me to wear in Columbus, Ohio.

I drove to Columbus and after checking into the hotel went to the ballroom to watch the competition which had just begun. At the door I was asked for my ticket.

"I paid my instructor."

But Brian O'Day had not yet arrived.

The doorkeeper eventually told me to talk to a gentleman who was standing at a door talking on the other side of the hall. I walked over there and told him my problem and he led me back to the first door and said, "Let her go in!"

I did not know then that this was Sam Sodono, famous as an instructor, coach, and organizer of the Ohio Star Competition, known as the premier dance event and at that time shown on national television.

We still greet each other as old friends and I have since reminded him of how we met.

My dancing in the competition was certainly not memorable but the professional performances, the expensive costumes, and the television cameras at all angles made the trip worthwhile. This was dancing excitement!

Back at the Mishawaka studio I continued dance lessons twice a week with Brian O'Day. I most enjoyed the socializing at the parties on Thursday and Sunday nights and participating in the group dance classes where I could meet and talk to the other students.

Dancing at a party with Dan O'Day

I made many friends and noticed that there would often be young single women who would join temporarily thinking this would be a good meeting place.

One of my friends lost her husband, a retired engineer, to one of these predatory women. He moved to their Lake Michigan cottage and his wife stayed in their South Bend home. The new couple had the audacity of attending several of the studio dances together.

"I'm not changing my social life because of him," my friend told me, "and I hope he freezes living in that summer cottage."

I saw another similar situation when a teacher and a student each broke up their marriages to be together.

I learned from those competitions, too. Politics, jealousy, arrogance, and favoritism are part of the dance world. Many dancers are serious competitors and are not always 'nice.' And, it's an expensive hobby.

My next competition was in Merrillville, Indiana. Many students from the studio participated there because it was a short driving distance and did not require professional clothing.

Dancing was always socializing for me. I loved seeing the beautiful dresses and listening to the variety of music. I loved the dress up dinners with a professional show. I loved talking to people from other studios.

For the next few years I did a variety of competitions. I drove to most locations and once took the train to Wisconsin where the train depot was just walking distance to the historic hotel. Some of us carpooled to one comp and I provided transportation for one student at a comp in downtown Nashville. Cleveland, Twin Cities, Chicago were some of the other locations.

And, of course, there was always Ohio Star. But I went there as a spectator only at that time. The televised shows were not shown live and one time I saw myself on national television sitting in the audience wearing my sparkly bright green dress. And always there was excitement, glamour, and socializing.

At one of the Ohio Star Competitions my reserved seat was near a group from Indianapolis who cheered loudly for Nicole Collins and Dan Rutherford who were competing in professional rhythm. I had no way of knowing then that they would eventually become good friends and make a difference in my life.

At that time I was very involved at the O'Day studio and had the goal of achieving the final silver level. Dan had a chart on the wall that showed the level of each student's dancing. We took tests to achieve each level. On the test we were judged by dancing each dance pattern alone and with our teacher. Then all those who had progressed would do a little showcase at a party to celebrate.

We sometimes had dance performance parties with someone outside the studio doing a critique to help us improve our skills. At one of these I was pleasantly surprised to see Dan Rutherford as the judge and I remembered him from Ohio Star. We talked and he invited me to attend dances at his studio in Indianapolis whenever I was visiting one of my children in the area.

But I was happy at the Dan O'Day studio. We enjoyed a special Year 2000 New Year's party with champagne and we toasted and danced in the new centennial.

In January 2001 many of us went on a dance cruise with the studio. We danced on a slightly swaying floor and all had a really . good time. One of the girls spent much of her time gambling and actually won money. But for the rest of us it was just fun.

I did enjoy an occasional party at the studio in Indianapolis.

This led, of course, to Dan asking me to take some dance lessons from him. What a difference it made to receive training from a top professional dancer! Rhythm, of course, had always been my favorite and easiest dance and the lesson experiences were beyond my wildest dreams.

That summer the Spohn Ballroom in Goshen was renovated in order to have a big dance extravaganza complete with orchestra and antique cars providing transportation. I was surprised to see Dan and Nicole there doing the professional show.

For the next few months I continued my lessons at the O'Day studio so that I could finally achieve my goal and pass the tests at the advanced silver level. And, of course, I would still enjoy my social life with friends there.

However, I would also make trips to Indianapolis for lessons in rhythm with Dan Rutherford

After doing a showcase at the Rutherford studio I was presented with the idea of dancing at a competition in Las Vegas. So, I met Dan and Nicole Carroll at the airport. And, we traveled together to the Stardust Hotel. Being with them at a comp I felt for the first time a part of the dance world. They were well known as top professional competitors. And I did a better job.

In Las Vegas with Dan Rutherford and Nicole Carroll

It was in Las Vegas that I became acquainted with Chris Ford who was there competing with another student.

Las Vegas was such a happy experience that I quickly agreed to the Hawaii comp. I had been to Hawaii before and anticipated a return.

Then came 9-11-01, a national tragedy. We had planned to meet at the airport for our long flight to Hawaii so I drove to Indy the day before.

My son answered the phone late at night. "You don't need to take your mother to the airport tomorrow. We have cancelled the trip. Many of the students are concerned about flying at this time."

Our alternate trip was to be the competition at Ohio Star.

So I returned to the Mishawaka studio and worked especially hard to fulfill my dream of passing the final silver level in dancing and to have my name moved to that area in the hall of the ballroom studio where all the members were categorized at their level. And I proudly danced a showcase there to celebrate this achievement which at one time seemed almost impossible.

At the Rutherford studio I did another showcase in preparation for Ohio Star. My progress there was beginning to require frequent lessons.

"You're spending so much time here in Indy. Why don't you move here?" questioned my friend, Chris Ford.

Chris Ford

Until then I had not given that a thought. I had lived in Elkhart County for forty years.

But then I considered, "Why not?" And I started house hunting.

Dancing in Ohio Star this time felt really good. I danced only rhythm, of course, and I know that I did the best that I had ever done at a competition.

Ohio Star Trophy

The beautiful historic Grove Park Inn in Ashville, North Carolina was the sight of my next competition. It proved to be a high point but although I didn't realize it at the time, the last of my fun competitions. We ate in the historic dining room and had views of the spacious landscaped grounds which looked out over a golf course and low hills. A swimming pool and health club were located in the basement and I bought one of their swim suits so that I could enjoy the pool with its waterfall.

While there some of us toured the Biltmore mansion. I enjoyed the Inn and Biltmore so much that a few years later I did a tourist trip in the area.

My next competition was in a suburb of Houston, Texas. My memory of that was that we sat in bleachers at the comp and I tore my expensive dress. Fortunately my friend Deirdre Baker who had made my dresses was also attending and she did a quick expert repair. I can't even locate the damaged area.

Returning to Indy I bought a house, sold my Elkhart house in one day and moved.

But after performing in the Indianapolis comp I lost interest in dancing competitions and in the Rutherford studio.

For a short time I joined another dance club in Indianapolis which had been recommended by Dan O'Day. They had fantastic parties but after doing a showcase with them I left ballroom dancing.

Years later my daughter, Linda, gave me a gift of two lessons with my friend, Chris Ford. My two sons and other daughter also each gave me dance gifts. This got me back into the sport I had loved. So, I have been enjoying one lesson a week for fun and I intend to continue this as long as I am able. I might actually do a showcase again but I have no desire to return to the competition life. My happy dancing days have really not come to a complete end. I still have many pleasant memories of a time in my life when I was really involved in the dance world.

RACE RELATIONS 101

"What's the matter with them people's faces?" I remember saying as a young child while my mother and I waited at a busy intersection in downtown Fort Wayne, Indiana. I don't recall what she answered but I do know that everyone in the small Indiana town where I grew up was white like me.

My next memory of someone of a different race was in the Fort Wayne department store where we shopped. The elevator operator was a black man who skillfully manipulated the post which stuck up from the floor with a big knob on top. He needed to manually adjust this at each floor. Then he would announce, "Second floor ladies wear, third floor housewares, and so forth. He could occasionally sit on the small stool in the corner. This was the only elevator I saw while growing up.

I remember once Mother saying, "They know their place," about some black people. I questioned her but don't remember the answer.

When I went south for college on the train I remember the rest rooms at the train depot. "Colored ladies" and "White ladies only." So I had to be careful to enter the correct door.

In college there were no black students but many black maids and yard workers. This was the teenage era of sunbathing on the roof. I remember thinking, "Why are we trying to be brown and maybe the brown workers would rather be white."

In later years my in-laws were renting a big house in town with an old slave cabin a few steps behind the back door. I went in it once and it had fading and peeling wallpaper but no furniture. They kept the building locked and not used. Riding throughout the countryside in those times I noticed many similar cabins.

My in-laws lived in the south and were very prejudiced. They were definitely not happy with school integration. As far as I know the family had never been slave owners but there was an atmosphere in the South that was different than in the North. My in-laws and their friends were good kind people and were active in their church and in the Masonic Lodge which is a Christian organization.

As a young child visiting my grandparents in Plymouth, Indiana we would occasionally drive past a large old brick house at the edge of town. I was told that it had belonged to my great, great grandfather and his brother who operated a brewery in the out buildings which at that time were next to the river. Throughout the years the Yellow River had changed course and was then further from the house. I was also told that the brewery and the house had been an underground railroad station during the Civil War.

When I was studying this in school I questioned my mother and grandmother but they were more proud of the fact that my great grandfather had owned and operated a hardware store in town and had been the first sheriff of Marshall County, evidently an important position at that time.

My mother's older sister told me about the house. She said that as a young child she had been in the basement and had seen the tunnel where the slaves had walked from the river and the brewery to achieve their freedom.

As an adult I decided to check this out and I stopped at the house and knocked on the door hoping that the present owner would let me see the entrance to this tunnel. The lady was very kind and also surprised when I told her the history. She made no offer of letting me view her basement.

A few years ago I went on a bus trip to visit the Underground Museum in Cincinnati. The whole museum is very well done and a tribute to the brave people who helped slaves escape and to those slaves.

I have a legacy of parents who were always kind and friendly to everyone and I am proud that my children have continued this behavior.

THE OLD MAIN STREET

"Unbelievable!" I thought, as I paused while looking through the 2010 Sunrise Cookbook, published for charity by Indy channel 13. It included recipes from outstanding restaurants throughout Indiana. And, the Main View Inn in North Manchester had a featured recipe for sugar cream pie.

Growing up I knew that place as 'the beer joint' and learned that respectable people did not patronize the establishment. I even felt a little guilty going by as I walked down Main Street to Louie's Candy Shop which was the teen hang out. Louie was friendly and greeted everyone who entered by name as he worked behind the ancient soda fountain preparing soft drinks and homemade ice cream. Or he would step across the store to weigh out the hand made candy. Lex, his wife, waitressed at the old wooden booths. And the jukebox played the latest big band music of the 40's. The noise of the music was joined with the sound of conversation and laughing of teenagers. I remember that Louie had control of the cash register and Lex just handed him the money and he would hand her the change for the customer.

After I left Louie's I might walk further west down the street to the Electric Store where I could purchase a 78 record of the latest swing band music to play on our record player in the living room at home. It was new and included a radio so we could listen to Amos and Andy, Jack Benny, and the news which were Daddy's choices in programs. I had a smaller radio in my room. Our one telephone was in the kitchen attached to the wall with a telephone book hanging on a nail next to it. Those were our modern means of communication.

Stores in town were very familiar to me. Because we had a business our family spent a lot of time down town. Then, when I was old enough to reach over the counter I learned to work at the soda fountain. Businessmen in town would take breaks from work to sit at the counter with soft drinks and talk about the town news.

On Saturday nights farmers and their families would come to town to do their weekly shopping and to socialize. Stores stayed open late. On Sunday all businesses were closed except for a few hours in the drug stores to provide medicine if needed and the Sunday newspapers.

Our house was located only a few blocks from downtown and I walked that short distance many times. As I approached Main Street I would pass Dr. Bunker's large Victorian house and then round the corner to pass the Wilcox Filling Station. Across the street was a car agency which was turned into a factory during the war. Then it was down the street past the monument shop with tomb stones lining the sidewalk next to the street. If I had passed Main Street and continued down Mill Street I would have been to the historic covered bridge.

The Covered Bridge, North Manchester, Indiana

But that was not my destination so I would turn the corner and walk west on Main Street.

Then I could look across at the furniture store on the corner and at Rufle Jewelry Store. Next was the American Legion Hall and the bank. As I walked west I would pass Strauss Feed Mill with feed in colorful print bags. Then it was two grocery stores, a five and ten cents store, and Urschel's with dry goods in the front and hardware in the back. Our family business, The Rexall Drug Store, was my final stop.

Sometimes I would walk from our store to the library. So I would cross Walnut Street and first pass the Walgreen Drug Store on the corner. Two movie theaters were next to each other. The Marshall Theater was on the site of Thomas Marshall's birth place and they ran the better quality movies. Ritz Theater had many cowboy movies. You could sometimes smell popcorn as you walked by.

Oppenheim's Department Store had two main entrances. One was for men's clothing and one was for women's with dry goods at the front and ready-to-wear at the back. On down the street was the telephone company and the News Journal newspaper office. Further down was Mike's Filling Station.

Across the street was the town hall, the police station, and the fire department with the one fire engine in view from under the building. Next to the fire station there was a road that led down a hill to a bridge over the Eel River. This led to the "pocket," a comfortable residential area.

Back down the street west of Mike's, a roller skating rink was in operation throughout much of my teenage years. I remember many happy hours skating to the music either alone or with a partner. Further down the street was the library.

At the store I would be asked many times to go to the post office for mail and stamps. Our mail at home was deposited in a mailbox by the front door by a mailman who walked his route, but businesses had a box at the post office.

So I would walk west around the corner of Gresso's Men's Store, down Walnut Street past the hardware store, and then by a car agency on the corner. Then across that street was the post office and to the west a photography studio. The post office building was fairly new and had a depression painting on the wall which was popular at that time.

On the remaining corner was the Sheller Hotel. I have pleasant members of the building and of Jane Sheller. During the war she prepared lunches in the dining room and my mother, my brother and I would sit at the same table each noon for lunch. We were only a few blocks from the junior and senior high school. I don't remember a menu, but I do remember eating delicious food, probably the same as she prepared for her two daughters who ate in the kitchen. She also catered for many social occasions through the years.

There were many more stores in town and I have only recounted the ones that were particularly memorable to me. Townspeople could have all their needs met by shopping in the downtown. Some did not have a car or need one.

Of course, my mother always felt the need to drive to Fort Wayne and to shop downtown at Wolf and Dessauer where they had more selections. But during the war their merchandise was very skimpy.

North Manchester is now a tourist attraction known as an historic town with many beautiful houses restored to their previous elegance. There is also a small park which is on top of the pioneer cemetery. Because there had been vandalism, the grave stones were moved to a pile in the corner. Thomas Marshall's house has been restored and moved to that location. Central junior and senior high school, adjoining the cemetery, has been demolished and a new library was built at that location to replace it.

Riding around town, many of the houses look familiar and I'm glad that everything looks well maintained. But memories crowd my mind of a time and good people gone forever.

The stores on Main Street and Walnut Street in the down town area look basically the same on the outside but with different names and merchandise. Only the Main View Inn, "The Old Beer Joint," has stayed the same. It now has an elegant menu which qualifies it for one of the top restaurants in Indiana according to the Sunrise Cookbook.

A NEW CHAPTER OF LIFE

"I'm going to a singles dance tonight and thought you might join me."

"Well, I don't know." The thought of two adult single teachers at a dance didn't seem desirable.

"You need to get out and see people. I'll pick you up in an hour and we can stop for a sandwich on the way."

And it was a dance at Studebaker Park in Elkhart. But unlike the room full of losers that I had expected, we had all experienced difficult times in our lives. But these people were enjoying life, making new friends, and overcoming various difficulties. Most important to me, I was receiving an acceptance and respect and immediately became a member of the group. This became a new chapter in my life and I looked forward to Friday nights after a long work week.

My friend, Nancy, did me two big favors. When I had dental problems and no dentist, she persuaded her high school friend, a dentist, to help me. And, she managed my membership in Parents Without Partners.

I started attending PWP meetings and dances in Elkhart and made many new friends. Then I learned that I could also attend activities in South Bend and that included camping trips. This started me on new adventures.

For my first camping experience I arrived early at the designated house to park and car pool. In addition to my bedding and a change of clothes I included a supply of spray for all insects both flying and crawling. What a surprise! In all my state park experiences I never saw a bug of any kind. In fact, all the parks are extremely clean and well maintained.

Our sleeping facilities included mostly tents but some had small campers. Food had been carefully planned in advance but if there was a restaurant just a short drive away we would eat our evening meal there. I eventually bought my own tent with a sleeping bag but it was fun sharing with a girl friend, sleeping on the ground and talking until late at night.

Mornings, Jack, who had been a cook in the Army, would announce that breakfast was ready. And, yes, it was a park community bathroom which was always clean.

Our days were spent hiking and talking and enjoying the beautiful scenery.

I especially liked Dunes State Park and Turkey Run State Park but each was different. We went canoeing in Pine River. I fell in the river and was glad that I knew how to swim.

For Super Bowl week-ends we would rent a cottage at the park but watched very little of the football game. The biggest problem was that we included more people than were supposedly allowed to stay in the cabin. The solution? Slips of paper with location of sleeping spots. I usually drew the floor.

I enjoyed many other activities with South Bend PWP. I learned to play dominoes for pennies and felt successful if I brought home a quarter. On Monday it was Happy Hour in the same location and then those who chose to do so would go to different restaurants for dinner. I enjoyed eating in almost every place in the city.

GETTING THE DOGS GROOMED

My daughter, Linda, had made an appointment to take my two golden retrievers to the groomer just a couple miles from my house. She drives a little red sports car which barely seats two people. If I ride with her she puts her purse in the trunk. So she planned to drive my car to the groomer. Problems ahead! My two dogs sat in the back seat of my car eagerly waiting for the ride. But the car would not start!!

"I'll call and cancel the appointment," I exclaimed..

"No," said my daughter. "Get a blanket or something and I'm taking them in my car."

"How?"

"One can sit on the floor and one on the seat."

When she returned I asked her about the trip to the groomer.

"Well, neither dog would sit on the floor. One sat on the seat smearing the window with her nose, and the other sat partially on the seat, across the console with her paws on my leg. The seat belt beeped and complained all the way. But I got them both in and told the groomer what I wanted because I didn't like the job they did the last time. I'm walking them home."

When we returned to retrieve the dogs I was left with a choice. Either she walked both of the dogs or we each walked a dog the long distance. I decided to walk, even crossing a busy intersection. But she ended up walking both of them because they walked together as close as they could. This was a new and scary experience. We walked on the sidewalk and then the trails, not sure exactly where we were going except that it was straight into the low setting winter sun. We were relieved when the Monon Center came into view and we knew that we would soon be home.

When we got home Linda said, "Don't give up those exercises at Prime Life. I can't believe you walked this far!"

Mutt Strut at the Indianapolis 500 Track –
We all four walked the 2.5 miles around

Printed in the United States
By Bookmasters